Backyard Big

Growing Food in Your Backyard

Jeffrey S. McLain

Preface

It was the mid-1970s, and I was in the back seat of the family Volkswagen van as we traveled from Lafayette to Brentwood, California. It was early summer and already a hot day in the East Bay. All the windows were open, and thick, dry wind blew in our faces as we drove down Interstate 680. We were going to pick fruit in Brentwood. We all waited in anticipation of the fresh fruit to come. I was looking forward to the treats—sweet, juicy peaches that melt in your mouth. Harvesting the fruit of someone else's labor—picking fresh fruit—was one of my favorite activities.

The town of Brentwood, affectionately known as the U-pick Capital, is home to scores of fruit and vegetable farms, many of which have operated for generations. The soil and ideal climate make for fruit and vegetable heaven. I don't remember too much about the town of Brentwood in the 1970s. In fact, I am not sure if there was much of a downtown or city as we know it today. It seemed like a very long drive to the middle of nowhere, with a series of orchards and farms spread far apart. But, in reality it was only forty miles away. Even though there were a lot of different fruit farms, we timed our visit specifically for picking peaches. When we arrive, we jump out of the van to get our buckets. After a quick safety briefing (not much, believe me), we head off to find a private row and the very best peach tree. As we walk through the orchard with discarded peaches and peach pits, we finally reach a full tree and descend upon it with vigor. Per protocol, we are discouraged from eating the product before paying for it. We feel guilty when we decide we must taste a little bit of the peaches. Those tastes grow larger as we proceed, eating one whole peach, then a few more, and even more after that. Soon we are stuffed with peaches. Suddenly, we get hot and are ready to head to the next farm to pick something else! We load the car and drive off with the aroma of peaches in the air.

I was raised in the small town of Lafayette, California. At the time, it was a commuter town known for its seclusion and suburban feel. My father commuted many years to San Francisco to work in a high-rise building. Lafayette is a part of the East Bay Area and the recipient of fresh fruits and vegetables grown in the Central Valley of California. California's Central Valley is a 450-mile-long region extending the majority of California's length and is bordered by the Pacific Coast Range and San Francisco Bay to the west and the Sierra Nevada Mountains to the east. The Central Valley is one of the most productive agricultural zones globally, leading the nation's production of many fruits and vegetables. Thus, fresh produce was the norm in the East Bay, just a short drive from the Central Valley. I moved in the 1990s and was adopted into the Central Valley breadbasket. Now, I have a backyard large enough to plant my own fruit trees and vegetables and produce my own food. Growing fruits and vegetables is challenging and rewarding, and my respect for farmers grows every day. It is the passion for growing one's own fruits and vegetables that inspired me to write this book.

I live in Lodi, in the Central Valley of California, and this book is aptly written based on the hot-summer Mediterranean climate of this region. The weather in the Central Valley of California is referenced by the U.S. Department of Agriculture (USDA) climate zone based on winter temperatures. The Lodi USDA zone is 9a or 9b, depending on which side of town you reside. The tips and techniques I offer will work well for any hot-summer Mediterranean region; however, temporal adjustments may be needed depending on your climate type.

This book helps backyard growers plan and harvest their bounty every month of the year. I've included some introductory chapters on gardening basics before getting into specific plants. All pictures included are taken by yours truly unless otherwise stated. In the first chapter, I present what I hope is a compelling list of reasons to grow your own food. I hope that I will convince the reader (you) that vegetable and fruit growing is worthwhile and healthy. The second chapter addresses the basic requirements and considerations for growing your own food. These basics include climate, sun, water, and soil. In Chapter three, I address the significant and economical aspects of composting. Composting is not required for growing your own food; however, it offers many benefits for you and the environment. Chapter four addresses fruit trees from a broad perspective and covers items such as planting requirements, pruning, rootstock, and other fruit tree needs. Following the fruit tree chapter is the vegetable chapter. In this chapter, I review some pros and cons of vegetable gardening. I include suggestions on the location of your vegetable garden, raised bed considerations, and other aspects specific to vegetables.

Chapter six covers common fruit and vegetables and their care needs. I typically don't grow all these fruits and vegetables every year. There are some plants that I will always grow and some that I will grow if I have room and time. For example, I will likely always plant tomatoes, squash, potatoes, peppers, garlic, onions, and cucumbers. These vegetables produce a huge bounty, are readily eaten by my family, and grow well in my area. I am a giant pumpkin grower and will cultivate a huge squash every year for entertainment. The other vegetables I plant, if I have room and time, include asparagus, carrots, beets, broccoli, cauliflower, cabbage, lettuce, and kale. These do well in my area (just about everything does); however, they are not enjoyed as much by my family. They are also grown at slightly different times than summer vegetables, and sometimes, I am not as active in the yard when it is planting time.

In Chapter seven, I bring the calendar together so you can plan your backyard growing. Vegetable and fruit growing is about timing. It has to do with when you plant, when and how you care for those plants, and when you harvest. Growing takes long-term planning to figure out what you want and when to harvest it. In this chapter, I provide monthly vegetable and fruit growing tasks as well as a to-do list. You can spread out your labor, planting, and harvesting throughout the year to get food most frequently. I am trying to avoid the case where you have three months of food in one month during the summer, for example, when all your tomatoes ripen in the first week of July. I think it's wise to spread food production throughout the year.

Chapter eight finishes the book with two very important tables. The first table shows the proper monthly periods to sow seeds or transplant plants. The second table illustrates the approximate monthly periods of fruit and vegetable ripening times.

Some vegetables taste awful to me, and some take up a lot of room or are just obnoxious to grow and may not be suitable for your situation. The artichoke is one such example for me. These vegetables are healthy and delicious tasting, but the plants get enormous. I also don't think they produce enough artichokes on one plant to deserve the space they use. In my garden, they will take up an entire raised bed. Thus, I did not include a description of artichokes. In addition, I omitted brussels sprouts. It's fun growing brussels sprouts because they look like miniature cabbages growing on a stock, and the history of this plant would be fun to write about; however, they seem prone to pests in my situation. They are not worth it to me. Celery, rhubarb, spinach, and corn also didn't make the cut in my book due to taste and space needs. In terms of vegetables, I will plant several of the same variety to maximize yield.

Fruit trees are very prolific in general, and I strive for variety. I like how fruits exhibit a wide variety of ripening times, so you can spread out your harvest much easier than vegetables. I try to grow most types of fruit trees, and I address many in this book. My big fruit producers include peaches, nectarines, apricots, cherries, apples, and hybrid types such as Pluots®. I included a summary of all these plus grapes, citrus, pears, and plums. I also summarized care for berries, although I don't grow them currently and have not figured out how to keep raccoons and birds from destroying them. There is no tropical fruit-growing information in this book for obvious reasons. I also didn't include nut trees. There are plenty of nut trees in my area. There is no need to grow more. I also included a bit of information about herbs. Herbs are not technically fruit or vegetables, but they are edible and a good addition to any garden.

The great thing about gardening fruits and vegetables is that you can plant what you want. The omission of certain types of fruits and vegetables in this book is by no means a statement that they are inferior. This is an equal-opportunity fruit and vegetable book!

Contents

Chapter One

Why Should I Grow my Own Food?

In my opinion, the first and most significant reason to grow your own food is to get outside. Gardening is a wonderful way to get outdoors and experience nature from the safety of your backyard. You can experience the song of birds at sunrise, the sound of the breeze through the trees, and the smell of soil. Planting, watering, digging, pruning, and weeding in the elements is therapy for the soul. It is no surprise that research continues to find only positive results from spending more time in nature. The effects of reduced time in nature are termed nature deficit disorder and it is a real problem. It is found to be related to obesity, high blood pressure, high cholesterol, and diabetes. This issue continues to trend upward as society spends less time outside. Obesity is especially a concerning trend in children. The more children sit on the couch and the less they play outdoors, the more obese they can become. There are also correlations between time outdoors and mental ailments, including autism and depression, and social and behavioral difficulties. All is not lost. Studies have shown that the nature deficit can be overcome with consistent increases in time in nature. Gardening is thought to be an effective way to spend time in nature.

Growing your own food in your backyard is actually a good form of exercise. It may not seem this way, but it really is. What about turning the soil in the garden patch, using a pick to dig out a tree stump, pruning bushes, or trimming your fruit trees? These are all activities that get you off the couch and into the sunshine. They help tone your muscles and improve your mobility. There is no doubt that heavy yard work will raise your heart rate. Try digging a hole in clay soil. As a former weightlifter, I used to spend hours lifting heavy things in the gym. In the yard, I lift things, swing things, and perform a variety of activities that not only help exercise my muscles but also produce results. It could be because I am getting older, but I am often sore the next day from heavy yard work.

Growing your own food can save you money. Retail prices for produce are increasing rapidly. The days of 10-cent lettuce heads are gone. For example, as of the date of this book, yellow onions are now more than $1 a pound on the West Coast in many stores. In some cases, they are nearly $2 per pound! It costs approximately two cents per onion transplant. Water costs a little bit, and fertilizer, if you wish to add that. That is a pretty handsome profit for one onion, approximately one pound (ca. 0.5 kilograms) in size. In addition, you don't have to pay for gas to pick up your onions at the store. Tomato and pepper plants may cost slightly more upfront; however, one plant can produce many fruits. What about a peach tree that produces 150 pounds (ca. 68 kilograms) of peaches? It may take some labor to prune your trees and spray them, but you would definitely make a profit.

Summer garden.

We all know that growing your own food results in better-tasting food. The tomato is a classic example. A tomato fresh picked from the plant, still warm from the sun, is just heaven. I have never purchased a tomato in a store that comes close to one grown in the garden. Even tomatoes sold as organic or on the vine in the grocery store don't compare. Another notable example is the peach. For transport to storage, peaches are often harvested when they are not ripe. Peaches that aren't ripe lack flavor. In the store, they are typically hard as a rock or overripened and mealy. When you grow peaches yourself, you can make sure you pick them at the peak of their ripeness. Also, you don't have to stress about damaging them during transport to your back door. I don't purchase peaches from the store anymore. There are many examples of fruits and vegetables that just taste better when grown yourself.

Of course, the fruits and vegetables that you've grown in your yard are fresh. They have not been stored or transported, adding time in the supply chain. You can leave your product on the plant until they are at the exact desired ripeness. If they are overripe, well, that is just your fault. But often, you can try your fruits or vegetables when you think they're ready. If they're not ready, just leave them on the plant longer. It's that easy. One of my favorite things to do is just walk out into the backyard, pick fruits and vegetables, and eat them right there.

Fruits and vegetables have their own natural beauty. Sure, they don't look like an elegant Japanese maple tree or sophisticated landscaping, but they can definitely compete with ornamental plants. A peach or plum tree just before leaf fall is spectacular. The bright oranges and yellows are just amazing. The blossoms of many fruit trees are equally delightful for the eyes. You can use fruit trees around the yard as accent plants, edging for lawns, or border plants. Vegetables exhibit a unique structure that contrasts with traditional landscaping. Onions and garlic, broccoli, and cauliflower all have their own unique shape and shade of green, adding to the variety of the landscape. As the saying goes, "variety is the spice of life." Variety makes your backyard look lush and pleasing.

Another really compelling reason to grow your own fruits and vegetables is that you are aware of exactly what you put in your food. You know if it is organic or not. If it was not organic, you are aware of exactly what was used to control the pests. You know you didn't overspray or overapply chemicals. While I always strive to be as organic as possible, sometimes there is a need to use chemicals. In these cases, I apply them strictly to label instructions. Of course, there are certain things I will never spray near my food, such as weed killers or other chemicals that can get into the soil and into the food that you're eating.

Think about how much gas you are saving when you grow your own fruits and vegetables. Many of our fruits and vegetables are shipped long distances, from field, to distribution center, then to our grocery stores, costing valuable fuel in the process. Fuel and transportation contribute to climate change and road congestion. Walking into the backyard, grabbing that food, walking back into the house, and eating offers significant benefits to the environment.

Growing your own food in your backyard is like having a classroom at your house. It provides fantastic opportunities to educate others about our food supply. In addition, visitors to your house will get tours of your food-growing operation. I particularly like giving tours to children who are amazed at what an onion plant looks like. This investment in the younger generation can help them save the environment.

Gardening is easier than one thinks and involves a lot of trial and error. The experts didn't just immediately start growing fruits and vegetables successfully. They failed, adjusted, and then tried again. Don't be discouraged by your failures. Learn from them and try again. Chances are that you have a patch of ground somewhere in the backyard of your house ready for some experimentation. It isn't an expensive hobby, and it is easy to experiment. Go ahead and give it a try.

Chapter Two

Climate, Sun, Water, and Soil

Plants need a particular climate range with a certain amount of sun, water, and soil to grow and produce food. I will cover the basics of each of these categories here. I am not going to get into the weeds, no pun intended, but I will give you enough information to get started and be successful at growing your own food.

Climate

Climate is a very serious consideration for your plants. Your fruit trees and vegetable plants have a certain amount of climate tolerance. The U.S. Department of Agriculture (USDA) has defined climate zones for reference. The climate zones are based on minimum winter temperatures. In addition, many are probably aware of the climate zones described in the Sunset Western Garden Book.[1] These climate zones are similar, although further adjusted from USDA climate zones by incorporating summer high temperatures, humidity, length of growing season, and other factors. Many variables affect climate, such as the distance from the equator, the elevation, the influence of the ocean, and the influence of winds and airflow. The climate can be very local. For example, my property tends to get several degrees colder than locations in town because air flows from the Sierras westward down into my quaint neck of the woods. This air settles in low spots. In addition, the temperature on the east side of my property at the chicken coop is usually three or more degrees cooler during the winter than on the west side of my house over the lawn. If your garden is close

---

1. 1995. *Sunset Western Garden Book.* Menlo Park, Calif., Sunset Pub. Corp.

to a sunny side of the house, such as a south-facing wall, it can get very hot in the afternoons in my region. As a result, you need to make sure that the plants you use can tolerate the climate zone in which you are planting them. Some plant labels actually have the climate zone on them, but unfortunately, most don't. You'll need to do a little bit of research in most cases. Many regions have a master gardener program with loads of local information and contacts for questions. If you're mindful of the frost dates, most vegetables you get for transplant can be grown in just about any region. However, some fruit trees don't do well in colder regions. For example, citrus trees do quite well in Southern California. However, in Northern California, they do grow, but may need some protection from frost, especially when they're young. The further north you go, the fewer citrus trees exist. I have always wanted to grow an avocado tree in Lodi. But much to my dismay, I just don't think it's possible. I've had friends give it a try. Some varieties supposedly survive, but many eventually die in the winter. To ensure success for your plants, know your climate zone and research the plants that will grow in it.

Sun

Obviously, plants need sun. The sun is converted into energy through photosynthesis. Without photosynthetic energy, your plants will not grow, and they won't produce your food! I tend to believe that you should provide as much sun as possible for your plants. That's why I try to find the sunniest spot possible when I plant them in my yard. Some plants can tolerate shade and will actually produce fruit and vegetables in some shade. Fruit trees need at least six hours of sunlight in almost every case. They say the same about vegetables. However, some vegetables can tolerate shade. In fact, some vegetables get too much sun. During such times, leaves burn, and fruit does not develop. For example, my giant pumpkin plants that I grow every year need to be shaded. When the temperature reaches over 100 degrees Fahrenheit (ca. 38 °C), leaves scorch, and pumpkins may even die if they are not protected enough. In general, I keep my pumpkin plants shaded the entire season. This is an example of where you can grow something in an area if it's technically not suitable for your particular climate zone. Pumpkins do well in cooler coastal climates. But many of us make do, and we can grow successful pumpkins with a little extra care. I have tried to indicate the need for sun levels in the descriptions of the fruits and vegetables in this book.

Water

I'm going to proceed with the term irrigation. Irrigation is the term used for the application of water to your plants. This is a very significant aspect to consider for your fruits and vegetables. Depending on the size of your lot, you may or may not have water access in your orchard or your vegetable garden. Fortunately, I have water access in both locations. However, I've had to do plenty of adjusting to make it more efficient. Here are some different types of irrigation systems, and the pros and cons of each, so that you can decide what works best for you.

First, there is hand watering with a hose. The most appealing thing about this approach is that you can give your plants the attention they deserve. It works wonderfully for vegetables, as it forces you into the garden at least once a day during the heat of the summer to water them. You can put just enough water on your plants. But not too much. Because you're watering your plants frequently, you can also check for pests and other problems. This is a benefit of hand watering, as you are forced to look at your plants. As a result of manual watering, you can monitor your plants more frequently and prevent problems. The disadvantage of the manual watering method is that you have to water them frequently; you have to remember, and you have to squeeze time into your schedule to get out there to water them. It is also common to provide water over the top of the plant. This is not a healthy thing to do for some types of plants that are more susceptible to diseases. The focus of your watering should be on the roots in these cases. Lastly, manual watering is not considered efficient, as the plant is commonly not able to absorb all of the water when it is applied at once, in such large quantities.

One way that uses water from a hose or through a trench system is flood irrigation. This old-fashioned way of watering crops with a trough is still used throughout the world today. You can mimic this type of environment in your vegetable garden. I often do this with my onions. I plant onions in elevated rows, allowing flood irrigation and quick drainage to avoid rotting. Of course, this does take manual labor and time to do, and it is not considered as water saving as our next method.

The next type of irrigation is drip. There are a lot of different types of drip systems. There is tubing with emitters with microsprayers or drips on them. There's drip tape or even soaker hoses.

These types of drip systems can even be planted under the ground. Drip irrigation will slowly provide water to your plant roots. This is considered water saving as well as beneficial to your plants. Commonly, drip systems come with some sort of timer associated with them. You can, however, just connect them to a hose bib. Turn them on and run them, and then turn them off when everything is wet, in this case. For fruit trees, this is probably the most suitable option. I use a drip system with emitters and run my drip system for the entire day, one day a week. There are plenty of places to purchase drip equipment, whether it's at your local hardware store or online.

In the final category, I mention sprinklers, such as rain bird types, and spray irrigators commonly used for shrubs and lawns. These can be used in vegetable gardens and orchards. For example, I often use a manual rotary sprinkler to water my pumpkin patch at certain times of the year. These are not water saving, however, and they can distribute a large amount of water across a large area relatively quickly.

A note about timers. They will allow you to water your plants when you are away, and in addition, they will keep watering them consistently when you are present. It may take you some time to figure out the right type of timer for your situation. If you have access to power nearby, you may want to pursue an electric timer. If you are too far from electricity, a battery-operated timer may be more suitable for your situation. Timers range widely in options and costs. You will need to consider how frequently you would like to water and how many different watering lines you would like to run from the timer. For example, one vegetable bed may need to be watered daily for two hours, yet your fruit trees might need weekly watering. I use a combination of hand watering and drip watering for my vegetables. I use an advanced timer on my pumpkin patch that runs misters at five- or ten-minute intervals during the heat of the day.

Soil

John Steinbeck wrote in The Grapes of Wrath, describing what happens when someone else raises your food for you. "And when that crop grew and was harvested, no man had crumbled a hot clod in his fingers and let the earth sift past his fingertips. No man had touched the seed or lusted for the growth. Men ate what they had not raised, had no connection with the bread. The land bore under iron, and under iron gradually died; for it was not loved or hated, it had no prayers or curses." Steinbeck was saying that you become disconnected from your land, and that you must be connected to your soil. You are a gardener now, and you are inextricably linked to your soil. Life comes from the soil. You will eat food that grows in your backyard soil. Soil is a wonderfully complex matter that deserves attention. You must take care of it. You inherit certain soil in your backyard, and you can't change that fact, but you can change your soil for the better. I spend a lot of time amending my soil with healthy things, taking care of it, and preserving it.

Soil is composed of four components: approximately 45% inorganic matter, 5% organic matter, 20%-30% water, and 20%-30% air. The first part of inorganic matter in soil is made up of rock, sand, silt, and clay. Of course, there can be boulders and large rocks, but these are not common in garden soil. Soil is classified by the different sizes of particles and the proportion of those particles. The primary particles are sand, silt, and clay. Sand particles are classified between 2.00 mm and 0.05 mm. Silt is anything between 0.05 mm and 0.002 mm, and clay is less than 0.002 mm. The proportion of these three elements will determine the type of soil you have. If you have too much of any one, you're going to have problems, but there is a way to mitigate the inadequacies.

You can do some simple tests at home to estimate how much of each of the three particles you have. Alternatively, you can send soil samples to labs to be tested. I test my soil every year to get an idea of how things are looking in my giant pumpkin patch. Last year, my soil was classified as clay loam, which, in my opinion, is very suitable. The ideal soil is approximately 40% sand, 40% silt, and 20% clay. When you have an ideal mixture like this, it is termed loam. Loam has efficient water drainage and allows air to enter the soil, yet it also holds moisture well. When there is too much sand, the spaces between the particles are too large, and water flows through too quickly as a result. When this happens, it is difficult to keep your soil hydrated and for plants to absorb nutrients. If there is too much clay and not enough sand, for example, the opposite happens. Water will pool up and the soil will become over saturated. Less oxygen is present in this case, resulting in less microbial life. Consequently, fewer nutrients can be absorbed by the roots in this case.

Other inorganic matter in soil includes macronutrients and micronutrients. These nutrients exist in healthy soil and are used by your plants if available. It can be necessary to augment your soil with macro and micronutrients to maintain a high intensity growing environment. The macronutrients you most commonly hear about are nitrogen (N), phosphorus (P), and potassium (K), and they are required for plant growth. These are the primary macronutrients. The fertilizer you purchase will be marked as the percentage of each of these three key ingredients. Nitrogen is essential for growth as it is involved in energy metabolism and protein synthesis. Plants can absorb nitrogen through their roots as nitrate or even on their leaves and stems. A helpful example of what nitrogen will do is when you apply it to your lawn. Your lawn will green up and begin to grow faster shortly after fertilizer application. Phosphorus supports root growth and energy transport. You need healthy roots to absorb nutrients and phosphorus to develop and grow. Potassium increases photosynthesis capacity, strengthens cell tissue, and helps absorb nitrates.

Secondary macronutrients include calcium, magnesium, and sulfur, and these, too, are needed for plant growth, but not in large quantities like primary macronutrients. Healthy, fertile soil will have these nutrients available for root absorption. These macronutrients can be depleted over time with heavy planting and become less available if your soil is not balanced. While it is easy to find primary macronutrient fertilizers, secondary macronutrient fertilizers are less common. Some plants are very sensitive to primary macronutrients and absolutely need them for healthy development. For example, calcium deficiencies can cause blossom-end rot in tomatoes and prevent pumpkins from developing. If you notice problems with your vegetables, it could be due to secondary macronutrient problems.

Micronutrients include boron, zinc, iron, manganese, copper, molybdenum, and chlorine. Again, these nutrients are present in your soil and are part of a fertile loam. If you maintain a healthy amount of organic matter, you are likely to be well stocked with micronutrients.

Detritus is composed of things such as expired plants and animal matter like fallen leaves, manure, dead insects, and leaf litter. This term describes all of the valuable stuff found in your soil. Much of the organic matter in soil comes from plant tissue at various stages of decomposition. This decomposed matter is either transformed into usable things, such as soil nutrients in the form of humus, or used as food for other organisms. Plant tissue releases nutrients into the soil in a way that plants can use. Think of a forest floor with centuries of leaves and branches built up. Mulch is extremely helpful in building up soil organic matter as you add detritus to soil starved of this substance because we don't garden on a forest floor. By providing mulch, you add valuable organic matter to your soil. You can't see it easily, but it happens!

Animals in your soil, such as earthworms, moles, gophers, snakes, and insects, all play a role in soil health. There are millions of insects that spend their entire lives in the soil. Earthworms, sowbugs, mites, centipedes, millipedes, and spiders live in the soil. Soil organisms play a critical role in decomposing organic materials and preparing the soil for plant growth. These animals and insects are susceptible to chemicals, and care must be taken to minimize chemical spray impacts on them. The organic garden has a huge advantage over the chemical-ridden garden in that the soil is alive and actively converting detritus into usable nutrients.

By far the most fascinating part of soil life is the microbial community. It is said that only one percent of soil microscopic creatures have been described and understood. The types of organisms include things such as nematodes, algae, amoebae, actinomycetes, bacteria, and fungi.

All these microbes play a valuable role in soil health. Nematodes help by regulating other soil organism populations, converting nutrients into plant-available forms, providing a food source for other soil organisms, and consuming other organisms. Algae fix nitrogen (prepare it for plants to absorb) improve soil fertility by preventing erosion and adding dead matter as nutrients. Amoebae control bacterial populations by eating them and keeping them in check. Actinomycetes play a major role in the recycling of nutrients in the soil, facilitating the breakdown of organic matter into usable forms of plant nutrients. Bacteria are incredibly numerous and help recycle nutrients as well. In addition, they improve soil structure by forming microaggregates in the soil by binding soil particles together with their secretions.

Have you ever worked in your soil and noticed a white mass that looked stringy? This is a sign of soil fungus. It looks like stringy white strands or fuzzy areas on the soil surface. These strands, called hyphae, are made up of long threads of microscopic fungus cells. This is a positive sign. There has been so much information about beneficial soil fungi recently that I almost view my soil as fungi! There are three types of fungi: (1) biological controllers; (2) ecosystem regulators; and (3) species participating in organic matter decomposition and compound transformations. As far as biological control is concerned, fungi can regulate diseases, pests, and other organisms. Their role as ecosystem regulators establishes soil structure. For gardeners, the last type of fungi plays a crucial role in organic matter decomposition and compound transformation! This third type of fungus benefits plant growth by creating a mutualistic relationship with plant roots. It assists with nutrient availability and cycling.

Mycorrhizal fungi form a symbiotic relationship with plant roots. As the fungi colonize the root system of a plant, increased water and nutrient absorption occur, resulting in enhanced root development and plant growth. As the plant provides carbohydrates for the fungi, it also protects against pathogens. Mycorrhizae fungi's presence in the soil in sufficient quantities will greatly increase root mass, which in turn leads to larger plants and higher yields. Professional vegetable growers, giant pumpkin growers, and hobbyists purchase quantities of mycorrhizal fungi and amend their soil as studies show substantial growth improvements.

My previous warning to the reader was to avoid chemicals in the garden that negatively affect soil organisms. In addition, certain soil nutrients can be negatively affected by soil tilling. For example, fungi can be particularly impacted by tilling. Bacteria can recover over time from tilling disturbances. When in doubt, leave the tiller out!

The sweet spot for plant growth is 60% water and 40% air in your soil's pores. It is obvious that water and air are essential for life, and you have a huge role in making things happen in the soil. If air or water is missing, plant death will soon occur. I hope, by now, you have realized how critical soil structure is to creating optimal conditions for water and air. If there is too much water (don't overwater), all the pore spaces are filled with water, and the soil becomes completely saturated, preventing the exchange of gases, including air. What happens is that carbon dioxide produced by living matter in the soil, including roots, can't escape, and you get anaerobic conditions. Alternatively, if the soil doesn't have enough water, it can exchange gases effectively but can't provide plants and animals with enough water. Since over watering is a common gardening mistake, special attention should be paid to the soil moisture in your garden.

Chapter Three

Composting

What is compost? Essentially, compost is humus. Humus is defined as the dark organic matter formed by the decomposition of plants and animals. The finished compost resembles humus as we compost the plant parts. By adding compost to your garden, you essentially add a slow-release fertilizer, supplying nutrients to your plants over time. You also improve the soil structure to help with water and nutrient retention, ensure sufficient aeration, and help with drainage. The compost adds nutrients to the soil that can be accessed by plants. I use my compost pretty much everywhere in my yard. I use it heavily in my vegetable beds, adding several inches of compost on top of my garden beds every year. As I strive to avoid rototilling, the compost will just sit on top of my garden beds while things last over the winter. I also add compost to my orchard and anywhere I feel I need better soil.

Composting is the practice of breaking down organic matter into usable soil. It goes hand in hand with all sorts of gardening, general yard work, and even cooking. As one participates in gardening, cleaning up leaves, trimming bushes, and mowing your lawn, you generate organic matter, providing ingredients for your compost. It is also possible to compost items found in your house, including coffee grounds, shredded paper, produce, excess vegetables and fruits, etc. Once a composter, always a composter! For example, before discarding, you can assess every item generated in your garden and house for potential composting. You will not look at your yard the same way again. I've been known to get crazy with composting and develop multiple piles in stages. Alternatively, you can go the minimal route and just make a small pile of compost in the corner of your yard. Composting is an organic thing to do. It breaks down organic matter that would otherwise be disposed of into usable soil and provides a valuable soil additive and a means to improve your soil. Thus, you will need to purchase less bagged soil for your garden and potentially fewer synthetic fertilizers. It is a win-win.

You will need to think about where to keep your compost pile. Usually, it's advisable to do this in a location that doesn't get full sun, as it will heat up too fast and dry out. Compost isn't the prettiest of things; most people, including myself, place it in corners and along the edges of the yard. It will also have some off-putting odors at times. You will be moving things from your kitchen and garden into your compost pile. You may not want to put the pile in the back 40 if you have one of those. They sell compost containers of many types, even those that rotate or tumble so that you have less work to do to aerate. I opt to use simple and inexpensive containers. You can even just create a pile if you have room.

To make compost, you need nitrogen, carbon, air, and water. To get your nitrogen and carbon, you must try to balance roughly equal parts of green and brown. Some composting materials have differing levels of carbon, and it is not worth tracking this closely, in my opinion. Simply strive for equal brown and green. For example, mix brown leaves with grass clippings. Of course, if you mix these together, you will get better results. I simply add items as they become available in my kitchen and yard. Sometimes, I will have more green than brown and vice versa, but it seems to even out eventually when I turn the pile. In addition, if you have a way of reducing the size of your pieces of composting materials, it will speed up the development of compost. For example, I almost always try to get my leaves off the lawn and chop them up with the lawnmower before I put them in the compost. I also run trimmings through a shredder at times to reduce matter. You also need to ensure there is sufficient water. Your pile should be like a moist sponge. Not soaking wet, but damp. Air is also a necessary ingredient, and this is why composters turn their piles to introduce air. You can still get compost if you don't turn the pile. It just takes longer. One note: if you've recently applied pesticides or chemicals to your lawns, fruit trees, or any of the items you are discarding, it is advisable to skip placing them in the compost pile.

Let's talk about the process. What actually happens, and how is compost actually made? The work is done primarily by bacteria. Once you get your pile established, low-temperature bacteria get to work breaking things down. These bacteria, called psychrophiles, do best at temperatures of approximately 55 degrees Fahrenheit (ca. 13 °C); however, they can even decompose at temperatures below this. This is good news, as you know your pile of compost has already been worked on before it warms up. If you have enough psychrophilic bacteria in your pile, the center of it will start to warm up. Once this happens, the mesophiles begin to do their work. They prefer temperatures between 68 degrees Fahrenheit (ca. 20 °C) and 86 degrees Fahrenheit (ca. 30 °C). Following this, the heat loving, thermophilic bacteria take over your pile. Other things will show up in your compost pile, such as fungi, nematodes, various types of spiders, centipedes, beetles, slugs, snails, and various worms. All of these are responsible for breaking down your compost. It is truly remarkable how this happens. This is where I will remind you that the size of your pile matters. Yes, size matters. I find I need to use a fairly large pile in order for it to retain heat and speed up the composting process. I suggest at least three feet (ca. 0.9 m) by three feet (ca. 0.9 m). These guys will generate a lot of heat. It is not uncommon for my compost piles to get over 170 degrees Fahrenheit (ca. 77 °C) at the peak. This will kill all those nasty seeds from weeds and other things that you don't want in your future soil. Keeping the temperatures high will help reduce the amount of time it takes for your compost to develop.

The work done by bacteria and the heat produced will quickly use up the air and moisture. This is where you must turn your pile and add water. If you were to turn your pile, getting oxygen into your compost every week in theory, you could have finished compost in a matter of weeks. I tend to turn my compost when I get a chance, which means every month or so. In addition, I throw stuff in my compost pile that is not very easily composted, such as redwood needles, pine needles, and large pieces of vegetable matter. These types of things don't compost quickly, but I don't find myself in a rush to make compost as quickly as possible. I would rather reduce waste as much as possible and avoid throwing things out. I do find it worthwhile to have some sort of compost bin. This will keep things in one place, keeping my piles a consistent size. To turn my compost or soil, I use a pitchfork. I also have a compost thermometer to monitor the temperature. Often, I will turn the compost pile when the temperature gets close to ambient, and it requires another boost of oxygen and moisture. When I turn it again, adding a bit of water, the temperature rises significantly.

There is one other variation of composting worth mentioning: worm composting or vermicomposting. Red worms can be acquired from worm farms and kept in bins or outside piles. These red worms will digest all types of yard waste. In return, they will produce highly beneficial worm castings containing minerals and elements used by plants. These worm castings can then be added to your garden soil. I have a small section of red worms in my yard, and I try to keep feeding them year round. They require moisture and food to eat, such as kitchen scraps. I focus the food on one side of the worm bed and then switch sides, leaving the worm castings on the former side where the food was. I can then grab the castings without the worms. These castings can be added to vegetable beds.

Chapter Four

Introduction to Fruit Trees

Many people have a lemon tree or a similar citrus tree in their backyard. Maybe it is in the corner of the yard and neglected until it needs pruning or harvesting. Or maybe it is a prominent evergreen tree taking center stage. Once a year, the fruit falls on the ground, and it becomes a nuisance. Because, after all, you only use a few lemons. Even lemon meringue pie only uses a few lemons. Did you know it is possible to grow a variety of fruit trees in your backyard? Yes, you can do it. You can grow many types of fruit trees. You can get fruit trees on semi-dwarf or dwarf root stock. That means the trees will not get too large and can fit in your backyard. Furthermore, you can prune them to size, keeping them a controlled seven or eight feet tall, or even smaller, if you would like. The great thing about fruit trees is that they give you fruit year after year, potentially for decades. If they do not produce fruit to your satisfaction, you can pull them out and put a different variety in the location. I have already mentioned that fruit trees provide nice beauty to your yard. As borders, screens, and landscape plants. Your orchard does not have to be like a traditional orchard with rows and rows of trees. For example, I have 28 fruit trees in my yard. There are a few patches where there are five or six trees, but for the most part, the trees surround my yard around the edges of the lawn. These trees vary from plum, cherry, pear, apple, apricot, peach, nectarine, and more. There are more than 34 varieties of fruit in my garden. How is it possible to have more varieties of fruit than fruit trees? Well, that is because I have several multi-grafted fruit trees that have several varieties on one trunk. Yes, it is possible. I will introduce the basics of fruit trees in this chapter and address varietal-specific topics later in this book.

Author with bare root fruit tree.

There are a few requirements to have fruit trees in your backyard. Number one, they do need an adequate amount of sun. At least six to eight hours is preferable. It is also advised to check your garden zone in order to determine the types of fruit trees you can plant in your backyard. There are many varieties, as well as those that are grafted onto a rootstock that favors certain types of conditions. For example, if you have consistently wet areas, you may want to try a rootstock that handles saturated soil well. Many trees also require what is called chill hours, which is a need to get a certain number of hours below 45 degrees Fahrenheit (ca. 7 °C) for them to appropriately enter dormancy for the winter. If they do not get enough chill hours, they will not become dormant and will not produce fruit. Of course, I am talking about non-tropical fruit trees here, not things like avocados, guavas, etc. There are more and more varieties of fruit trees that are coming out that have very low chill requirements. This makes it easy to grow them in just about every location. In my location, there are enough chill hours to cultivate just about every type of fruit tree. In fact, less than a mile from my house, there are several successful commercial apple and cherry farms, not to mention almonds and other fruits. On the other hand, it is very difficult to grow tropical fruit trees in my area, such as avocado, banana, and mango, due to the cold winters.

You can get fruit trees just about anywhere they sell trees and can get them at any time of the year in most cases. Furthermore, you can plant them anytime you would plant a normal tree when the soil is somewhat warm. However, fruit trees come bare root during the dormant winter season, and this is an ideal time to purchase and plant. I believe it is more beneficial to plant fruit trees during the dormant season. For example, dormant bare root fruit trees are less susceptible to a number of problems that container fruit trees are susceptible to. Difficulties with container-planted trees include the potential to dry out, concerns with becoming root bound, etc. You can get dormant fruit trees at nurseries around December or January in my area. Sometimes, they are wrapped in a small burlap sack, and sometimes, they are planted in pots. They seem to take really well once you put them in the ground. I highly recommend Dave Wilson Nursery. They are located in Northern California and grow trees for nurseries and commercial businesses. In fact, Dave Wilson Nursery produces almond trees for almond growers, walnuts—you name it. But they also sell to nurseries and have very distinct genetic lines of fruit trees. Many trees are self fruitful, meaning that they don't require cross pollination with another fruit tree to produce fruit. All respectable fruit trees are labeled as self fruitful or not. If your fruit trees are not self fruitful, it is suggested to plant at least two compatible pollen varieties approximately 100 feet (ca. 30 m) apart for pollination purposes. Note that pollination will occur if the trees are closer and further than this guideline.

To plant a fruit tree, it is not necessary to dig a large hole or to fertilize when planting. If your tree is in a pot, dig a hole about as deep as the pot and twice as wide. Plant your tree in your soil, making sure not to bury it too deep. It should be planted at the same depth as it is in the pot. If planting a bare root tree, dig deep enough to bury the tree just above the roots and well below the graft union. Make sure the hole is plenty wide and spread the roots outward. Bury it with native soil. I stake all my trees for the first year to prevent wind damage. Planting time is a good time to do this.

Fruit trees do require maintenance. First, they should be pruned every year, at the proper time, to adjust the shape and structure of the tree and to remove damaged or diseased limbs. By pruning properly, you will also improve airflow through your tree and make harvesting easier. In addition to dormant season pruning, you may find it worthwhile to summer prune your fruit trees to control their size. It is wise to invest in a sharp pair of pruners, loppers, and a pruning saw. Research proper pruning techniques in books or online before your first pruning.

Unlike a vegetable garden that can be watered by hand, it is advisable to set up an irrigation system for your fruit trees. To irrigate my trees, I use drip lines that connect to my garden hose. It is also recommended that you mulch under your fruit trees to help with soil structure and retain moisture. You will also have to pick at least two times per season. First, early in the season, it is advisable to thin the fruit on your trees, and of course, you should pick your fruit when it is ready for harvest.

Finally, you will need to invest in a garden sprayer to spray your trees from time to time. In most cases, you can use all organic and spray with neem oil or horticultural oil. In other cases, you may need to apply pesticides or fungicides. I find I can mostly stay organic with my fruit trees, except for my peaches and nectarines, which I must spray copper for leaf curl. There are a variety of sprayer types available, from low-end hand pump sprayers to battery-operated sprayers on wheels and more. If you manage to keep your fruit trees small, you can get by with a hand sprayer like I do.

I recommend labeling all your trees in order to be aware of the exact type of fruit. You would be surprised at how similar trees and their fruit look in some cases, and a good identification will afford you all the necessary clues for care, ripeness dates, and other factors. I have tried all types of labels. Beware of attaching your labels to trees with wires, as the tree will grow around the wire before you know it. I find the best method is to use twine and durable metal tags as labels and use metal stamping equipment to mark them. These are durable, lasting years. I put the type of tree on one side and stamp the ripeness date on the other.

I plant mostly Dave Wilson Nursery brand fruit trees on semi-dwarf stock, and I strive for a variety that provides successive ripening so that I always have something coming during the season—between March and November. I keep my trees at a manageable height of approximately eight feet (ca. 2.4 m). In some areas where I need screens or privacy, I let them grow. I have a pear tree that is upwards of 25 feet (ca. 8 m). It depends somewhat on where the tree is.

Weeds can impact the health of your orchard as they can harbor insects, take nutrients, and are unsightly. I find I do not have much of a weed problem, as my yearly mulching routine keeps most weeds from growing. On occasion, if I do see a weed, I pull it. It is that simple. If there is a particular control problem with weeds in my orchard, I will spray with herbicide; however, this is not common.

Chapter Five

Introduction to Vegetables

You've just read an introductory chapter about fruit trees, so it seems appropriate to include a chapter about vegetables. Vegetables are different from fruit trees for several reasons. They have some advantages over fruit trees. For example, most vegetables are annuals, and if they do not work out, you can just pull them out and replace them. It is more challenging to do this with fruit trees. Vegetables are relatively inexpensive, and, in most cases, you do not have to prune a vegetable! You can get many types of vegetables and put them in one garden bed. If they grow well, you can plant more the following season. Some vegetables can even ripen multiple times in one season. In fact, some vegetables can produce food almost the entire year. Lettuce is an example of such a vegetable. While fruit tends to have ripening seasons mostly during the summer and fall, the vegetable garden can be tremendously productive almost all year. Vegetables can be frustrating at times as they are small and delicate plants. For example, you just planted a row of beautiful-looking lettuce only to find that a rabbit ate all of it overnight. Or your prize-winning tomatoes have blossom-end rot. Yes, vegetables can be tricky. Fruit trees tend to have problems, of course, but vegetables can get taken out quickly by a pest or disease.

You will need to decide where to cultivate your vegetables. I recommend growing them all in one location, as you will want to be efficient with your tools and watering in one area. It is also helpful to grow your vegetables close to the house so that you can harvest them and walk right into the kitchen. Ideally, it should be close to your compost pile so that you can toss the discards into the pile and also use the compost in your garden beds. Just like fruit trees, vegetables need lots of sun, so make sure you have a sunny location.

Will you be an indoor seed starter, outdoor seed starter, or will you purchase your plants as transplants? Starting seeds indoors takes time and effort. You will need adequate lighting and, depending on your indoor conditions, a heat mat, to keep the seedlings warm. Another thing you can do to make your indoor seed starting more successful, is to gradually introduce the young plants outside during warm days to help them get accustomed to wind and weather fluctuations. This is termed hardening off and helps prevent plant shock when you transplant them. You can find virtually any type of seed online, and you have many more choices for your vegetables if you sow them. If you direct seed outdoors, you run the risk of pests, such as birds and snails, eating your seedling sprouts when they are small and delicate. Purchasing transplants at the nursery is typically the most expensive method; however, may be your best chances for success.

Raised beds are a wonderful invention. People grow their vegetables in raised beds for a variety of reasons. First among them is raised beds allow you to cultivate the soil by adding conditioned topsoil without worrying about weeds. Raised beds also separate your vegetables from the ground, which helps to avoid pests. Temperature control is important for vegetables. Raised beds offer superior drainage, protection from the wind, and can heat up faster in the spring for your summer garden preparation. Some use raised beds for convenience, making them high enough, so you do not have to lean over too much to do your gardening. You can also make mulched or gravel pathways between your raised beds.

Raised beds can be rather expensive. If you choose to make them yourself, you'll find lumber is not cheap. You can also order prefabricated raised beds and have them delivered. Either way, the cost of gardening increases as a result of these factors. Of course, you can just go to a bare spot in your yard and plant vegetables there as well. I find I am far more successful with raised beds. There are plenty of ways to build raised beds on the cheap.

A special note about weeds. I do feel differently about weeds in my vegetable beds as opposed to my orchard. I can cover them with mulch in the orchard; however, in the garden, control of weeds is more imperative as they will steal nutrients and water from the vegetables. Your vegetables are shallow rooted, and so are the weeds. Unlike an orchard where fruit trees can grow deep for nutrients, vegetables cannot. Thus, I do a lot of weed pulling in my raised beds. Under no circumstances do I spray herbicides in my raised beds. I try to keep up and pull weeds frequently during the wet winter and spring.

Chapter Six

Select Fruits and Vegetables

APPLES

The apple is definitely the most common fruit worldwide. Everyone knows of apples, and everyone knows of the many sayings about apples, from, "an apple a day keeps the doctor away" to "the apple of my eye." Perhaps what is so unique about apples is that they can be stored for such a long period of time. Apples have hardened skins that enable them to withstand the elements and stay on the tree getting ripe. They can be picked early, stored, and eaten months later. Although I would not recommend eating an apple that is years old, sometimes I wonder how old the apples are at the grocery store. There are approximately 7,500 varieties of apples in the world and over 2,500 varieties in the United States. That is a lot of variety!

Apples have some chill hour requirements; however, they are one of the easiest trees to grow as they can do well in almost any soil type. Apple trees survive very low temperatures, high winds, and just about anything nature will throw at them. Even though they are hardy, apple trees prefer fertile, well-drained soil. Some rootstocks can be used to deal with saturated soil if this is a problem. There are many self-fertile apple trees, although it is generally recommended to have at least two apple trees that will pollinate each other to ensure a good harvest.

Green apples.

There are two basic types of apple trees: spur-type and non-spur. Spur-types grow differently than the normal fruit tree. They have fewer limbs and have these short, stubby, wrinkled stems on their branches. Spur-types will produce more apples and need less pruning. It is possible to head back branches to produce more spurs and, thus, fruit. Non-spur types lack those wrinkled stems and can handle heavy pruning like normal fruit trees. It is useful to know which type of tree you have so that you can prune it correctly.

Many apple tree designs can be achieved. They do well as espaliers, bushes, or trees with a central leader. You should heavily prune apple trees the first few years to get your plant's design figured out, whether in dormant season or not. These trees will grow quickly, so you will want to plan ahead. A standard tree can grow up to 35 feet (ca. 10 m) tall, a semi-dwarf 20 feet (ca. 6 m), and a dwarf 10 feet (ca. 3 m).

I have experienced two problems with apple trees. The first problem is codling moths. These moths can be a major problem with apples, and unfortunately, I got a good infestation one year. The moths lay eggs all over the trees; on the fruit, leaves, and bark. The larvae burrow into the fruit and feed mostly on the seeds. You can usually notice a little hole near the center of the apple. The next stage is the pupa, which resides in a cocoon. Finally, the moth is out and about to make more! These are very difficult to control with spray; however, I was able to get a handle on this problem by covering each of my apples with little protective covers resembling miniature stockings, preventing the larvae from burrowing into them. It took some time, but it was a good organic solution. Other solutions include pheromone traps to detect and remove the moths and tightly timed spraying. The other challenging disease I have had to manage is fireblight. Fireblight is a destructive, highly infectious disease caused by a bacterium. The bark of blighted twigs becomes water soaked and turns a dark color. Young twigs and branches die from the terminal end and appear burned or deep rust colored. Branches may be bent, resembling what is commonly referred to as a shepherd's crook. The best thing to do when you see a fireblight infection is to immediately cut below the branch, a minimum of two feet, or to the nearest joint. The sick branch should be discarded, not composted. This will prevent the ooze from dripping to other parts of the tree, infecting other branches, or being transmitted to nearby trees. Some apples are highly susceptible to fireblight. Some are resistant, but not completely. It is possible to spray for fireblight, but I have never attempted such a thing.

I enjoy my Hudson's Golden Gem apple as it has fireblight resistance, good-tasting apples, and is a fast grower. I have a tasty Golden Delicious apple that helps pollinate my Hudson's Golden Gem. The Golden Delicious apple is a yellow apple that is sweet and juicy and just fabulous for your daily apple. I also have another apple tree in my yard pruned as an espalier; however, I do not know the variety. I generally label all of my trees, yet for some reason, this tree was missed.

***

APRICOTS

Apricots are sometimes lumped with peaches and nectarines; however, they are unique enough, in my opinion, that they should be separate. They typically ripen earlier than peaches, nectarines, and other fruit, often making them one of the first summer fruit delights. Once they ripen, they spoil relatively quickly. They don't store long, and the ripeness window is pretty short. Harvest them on the right day, and they are delightful. I appreciate apricots because they appear to be less desirable to pests such as birds and raccoons.

Apricots

Apricot trees need plenty of sun and well drained, loamy soil. These trees grow rapidly, and keeping them small can be challenging. I often cut five feet (ca. 1.5 m) to 10 feet (ca. 3 m) off of my apricot trees every year during the summer. Sometimes, I fit in two summer pruning sessions. They are just vigorous trees. Apricots should not be pruned during the dormant season, and this is one reason why I didn't include them with peaches and nectarines. Pruning during the dormant season will cause open wounds, and these make them susceptible to diseases. Ideally, it is recommended to only prune them during the summer. Summer pruning is best while the apricots are still actively growing, and they can heal from their wounds quickly. Also, you can do a lot with apricots in terms of plant form. You can prune them like trees with open centers; you can make espalier fans, bush types of trees, and all types of shapes and sizes.

Apricots are typically ready for harvest in mid-May through mid-July in the Central Valley of California. There are a few apricots that are ready for harvest in August, such as the Puget Gold or the Autumn Gold. I am currently growing three types of apricots. Of course, all three are Dave Wilson Nursery brands. I have the Royal Rosa, the Katy Flavor, and the Tomcot. My Tomcot apricot grows so rapidly and produces so many apricots; it is an absolute blessing. It ripens in mid-June, pretty much before my peaches and nectarines, and it's my first real taste of an abundance of fruit for the summer, along with my cherries. The Katy apricot will also ripen in June; however, that tree is not as productive as the Tomcot. At least not yet; it's younger. There are a few dozen different types of apricots. I would encourage you to look around and find one that works best for you. The key is to have fruit coming all summer long.

ASPARAGUS

Starting in the late-1800s, the peat soils of California's Sacramento-San Joaquin Delta were home to significant asparagus crops. The Sacramento-San Joaquin Delta was an asparagus leader between the late-1800s and late-1900s; however, it appears they have mostly been replaced by an international market.

Asparagus can be added to many dishes, such as omelets, casseroles, pastas, salads, and stir-fries. You can even have them on their own as a side dish. Asparagus is packed with nutrients, low in cholesterol, fat, and sodium, and contains the antioxidants known to provide anticancer benefits. Asparagus roots are used as medicine for a variety of ailments, such as depression, poor milk production, and stress. What an impressive vegetable!

Perhaps one of the most beneficial things about asparagus is that it is ready for harvest at the beginning of spring before many other fruits and vegetables, filling the table with fresh produce before the bounty starts. Asparagus plants are perennials, can live up to 15 years, and have an exceptional growth habit. Most people start their asparagus with rhizomes called crowns. The tendency is to call these crowns roots, but they are actually fleshy stems with little roots attached. The crowns are planted in the soil when they are one or two years old, either in winter or early spring. Spears begin to pop through the soil the following spring, and the first-year spears should not be harvested. Following the spears, fernlike matter will grow several feet tall. This fernlike matter should be grown to provide nutrition for the plant and then cut off in the autumn. If you are short on space in the garden and can't handle having valuable real estate taken year round, asparagus may not be for you!

Asparagus do best in full sun and raised beds, but can tolerate some shade too. Well-fortified soil is a must. They thrive when the soil is slightly on the acidic side, between a pH of 6.5 and 7.0. This is a common range for most gardens, especially if fortified with compost. Do not plant asparagus in soggy soil. Newly planted asparagus needs approximately one to two inches of water a week. Asparagus are planted in late winter or early spring as the soil starts to warm up. Crowns should be planted approximately 10 inches (ca. 25 cm) to 12 inches (ca. 30 cm) deep in rows 12 inches (ca. 30 cm) to 18 inches (ca. 46 cm) apart that are approximately four feet (ca. 1.2 m) between rows. Use plenty of mulch, placing it on top of the rows. In the first year, you should let the spears develop and collect

Asparagus. Photo by Rick Whittle.

sunlight. The fernlike part of the plant will get fairly large and should be cut at the soil level during autumn, as this part of the plant is thought to harbor pests. Harvest begins in spring, and all spears should be cut at the surface, taking care not to damage the crown under the soil.

Weeds are not your asparagus' friends. You must keep a weed-free bed, or they will rob the plants of nutrients. Mulch is the best weed prohibition, and I recommend hand pulling. Resist the temptation to spray anything on your asparagus bed to control weeds! There are various pests that can cause havoc, particularly asparagus beetles and aphids; however, I have not had such bad luck as to be impacted by these pests. Floating row covers can help control pests as well as the early harvesting of the fernlike parts of the plant. Chemicals are a last resort.

Asparagus plants are either male or female, and males are the most popular as they are the most productive and easiest to harvest. There are more than a dozen varieties to grow in your home garden. Some are purple, white, and, of course, green. I would suggest selecting a variety that works best in your area. In California, green De Paloi and UC157 seem to be the reigning varieties, as they have good disease resistance and are well adapted to the climate.

BEETS

Beets. Photo by Markus Spiske.

You either hate or love beets. There is no in between. They taste like dirt, smell earthy, and they make your urine and fecal matter red. I am an official beet lover. My favorite is cooked beets in a salad, as well as beet juice decanted with apple juice! Beets are very nutritious. They are packed with antioxidants, anti-inflammatory nutrients, and are high in fiber. You can do a ton with beets. Try them baked, pickled, sautéed, juiced, boiled, or even raw. Add beet leaves to salads and side dishes, and take advantage of these highly nutritious gems.

Beets need full sun but do like cool weather. They are best sown in February or March or between August and October to afford growth during the cooler parts of the season. They can also be transplanted; however, most growers plant them by seed. Beets like soil that is loosely dug for fast root development. Sow seeds in rows approximately 0.5 inches (ca. 1.3 cm) deep. Each row should be approximately 12 inches (ca. 30 cm) to 18 inches (ca. 46 cm) apart. Once the seeds germinate and the little beets get a few inches long, thin them to leave one beet plant per three or four inches (ca. 8 to 10 cm). I find it relatively easy to start beets from seed; however, they can take up to two weeks to germinate when cold and are particularly susceptible to bird predation when they start. Speaking of pest and disease problems, my number one pest is—you named it—birds. They will be ready to chop those leaves right off when they germinate, so row covers or bird netting are a must. Beets typically grow during the cooler months when disease and most pest pressure is low. Nevertheless, if you experience issues, it can be related to soil deficiencies, overcrowding, and other cultural practices. See your local master gardener program or gardening club for information to troubleshoot.

Beets come in a variety of sizes and colors and are primarily categorized by their shapes. Types include globed, cylindrical, and semi- globe. Common varieties for home gardening in California include Ruby Queen, Detroit Dark Red, Early Wonder, and Burpee's Golden Beet. My go to is the Early Wonder.

***

BERRIES

Berries are a large and challenging group to summarize. There are blueberries, blackberries, strawberries, raspberries, loganberries, marionberries, gooseberries, elderberries, and so on. Berries are an excellent choice for backyard fruit. They don't get large like fruit trees do; they start to produce fruit quickly after planting, and they don't take a lot of care, such as significant pruning.

One thing I like about berries is that many of them have North American roots. For example, the strawberry has been eaten around the world in its native form for centuries. But it wasn't until the North American strawberry variety was bred and changed that the berry finally became the strawberry we know today—large, sweet, juicy berries. The blueberry is also native to North America, and although it was eaten by Native Americans and likely across the world, it wasn't until fairly recently that the North American blueberry cultivar was successfully used in the production of blueberries we know today. Many of you might see the occasional wild blueberry along creeks in California. Wild blueberries like moist conditions, and they like the riparian zone adjacent to creeks and streams. Blackberries consist of native North American varieties as well as European varieties. In order for me to cover this wide assortment of berries, I will address the more popular varieties one at a time below.

Strawberries

Two basic types of strawberries exist: short-day types and day-neutral types. The short-day types, as its name suggests, grow when the days get shorter in the fall, winter, or even early spring. The day-neutral types don't care about the length of the day and produce almost all year long except for some hot summer periods. The day-neutral types are also termed ever-bearing. In California, there are also two basic planting methods. Winter planting is commonly done in mild areas, such as coastal climates. In these cases, the plants start growing immediately after planting. In the interior valleys and warmer regions, summer plantings are typically done. These are planted in late summer and develop over the fall and winter. Fruit production starts in the summer.

Plant strawberries in sandy, well-draining soil about eight inches (ca. 20 cm) to 15 inches (ca. 38 cm) apart in rows. The row should be approximately six inches (ca. 15 cm) high and 12 inches (ca. 30 cm) to 18 inches (ca. 46 cm) wide. Strawberries have shallow roots, meaning they need lots of consistent water. Strawberries take to fertilization well, and I would recommend organic fertilizer, such as manure or compost. The plants will send out runners, and they should be cut off as they will take the energy from the main plant. Pests include birds, insects, slugs, and diseases. Bird netting is a good idea. You can control aphids, mites, and other insects organically or chemically as a last resort. The same goes for diseases; however, in severe cases, I recommend ripping out the plants, moving to a new location, and trying again. While you are at it, I would give different types a try. Some strawberries will work better in your backyard than others. Good short-day varieties are Douglas Pajaro, Shandler, Camarosa, or Sequoia. The neutral types to consider include Silva Muir, Irvine, Fern, and Hecker.

Blueberries

Blueberries grow on bushes and can add considerable beauty to the landscape. They will have many flowers during the summer and dark red leaves during the fall. Not to mention, they have pretty little berries that taste amazing. There are two basic types: lowbush and highbush. Of course, there are hybrids, adding to all the confusion. Lowbush types generally don't grow over 18 inches (ca. 46 cm) and are cold hardy. These are typically grown in areas of the Northeastern U.S. The small height of these plants makes them well adapted to handle snow. Highbush is like they sound. They get as tall as eight feet (ca. 2.4 m) in some varieties. These don't handle cold as well and can even handle a little drought. This is the variety of choice in hot inland regions.

Blueberries.

Blueberries require sun with well-drained soil, and they have a demand for soil pH between 4.5 and 5.5, which is lower than typical gardens. However, you can do things about this. Possible solutions include applications of sulfur or aluminum sulfate. The best time to plant two to three-year-old plants in pots is fall through winter. You can plant from potted blueberries, or you can plant bare roots. In my area, bare roots show up in nurseries prior to fruit trees, usually around December. These plants should be planted between eight (ca. 2.4 m) and 10 feet (ca. 3 m) apart if going directly into the ground. It is also possible to grow berries in pots. However, you must be mindful of watering. They have to stay moist, or they will suffer. Blueberries need a good amount of water, particularly during the summer. They require one to two inches of water a week during the hot months. Winter pruning is important to spur growth, and you should prune approximately 30% of a plant each year. Fruit production is on one-year-old vegetation.

Few pests are problematic except birds. Boy, birds love berries. They seem to have a good knack for finding them. Bird netting is highly recommended if you intend to see any edible blueberries. Highbush varieties of inland areas of California that are successful include Misty, Jubilee, O'Neal, and others.

Blackberries and Raspberries

Blackberries and raspberries are part of a group called brambles. Brambles are shrubs that grow with branches called canes. They commonly have prickles along their canes. Roses are even brambles. Long sleeves and gloves are the mainstay when you are working with brambles, for obvious reasons. You can plant brambles from pots or from bare roots. Planting is best done between late fall and early spring. Brambles like fertilized soil with a pH of 5.5 to 6.5. There are two types of plants:

trailing types that spread out by sending runners and long vines, or erect, upright types. If you are planting a trailing type, space them approximately five feet (ca. 1.5 m) apart. It is best to build a trellis for support. If it's an upright type, you can get away with using a stake, and you can plant them two feet (ca. 0.6 m) apart. There are self-fruitful varieties and some that need cross pollination.

Water thoroughly after planting and keep the soil moist. Brambles need one to two inches of water a week during the warmer months. Make sure to keep the soil moist but not muddy. Add more water during heat spells, windy conditions, or fruit development.

In order to understand the care and pruning of brambles, one must understand the different types of branches or canes, called primocanes and floricanes. The primocane is a cane growing in its first season of growth, and these canes typically flower but produce few fruits. Floricanes are second-year canes that produce the most fruit. Floricanes are done following their production during the second year and should be pruned. Furthermore, pruning of erect types of blackberries consists of pinching off several inches of the primocanes when they get approximately three feet (ca. 0.9 m) long to produce branches that will produce fruit the following year. Trailing blackberries will produce primocanes that lay along the ground the first year. You should prune out your floricanes and then set your primocanes on the trellis system. (Remember, you set up a fancy trellis system?)

The most common pests of brambles include mites, horntails (a worm), and crown borers. Common diseases include verticillium wilt, root rot, rust, leaf spot, and crown gall. Good sources about pests and diseases of blackberries can be found in university publications and in local master gardener information. The worst pest experience I had with brambles was with raccoons. These pests arrived exactly when my berries ripened and would walk over the plants, smashing them down, and devouring every last berry. The only raccoon deterrent that worked was bird netting propped up and suspended over the plants. Raccoons could eat through netting if they wanted to, but in most cases, they would seek something else to eat.

There are many varieties of erect and trailing blackberries, and I suggest checking for cultivars in your area. Popular varieties of inland California include the thornless Arapaho (erect), the thornless Triple Crown (semi-erect), and the thornless vigorously growing Black Diamond (trailing). Raspberries mostly do best in cooler coastal environments; however, there are a few varieties that work well in inland California, including Bababerry and Oregon 1030. If you can offer afternoon shade, you can open up the possibility of varieties. It is suggested to check cultivars in your area to find the best chance of success. Raspberries are not just red; they are also purple, black, and yellow as well.

***

BROCCOLI

"I do not like broccoli. And I haven't liked it since I was a little kid and my mother made me eat it. And I'm President of the United States, and I'm not going to eat any more broccoli." George W. Bush, former President of the United States. Like beets, you either hate broccoli or like it, but you can't deny that it has excellent nutritional value. You can hide it under sauce, cook it down to a mush, and do all kinds of things to it to get it down the hatch.

It is likely that the nutritional value of broccoli was the reason it became as popular as it is. Unlike many fruits and vegetables that are rumored to have medical benefits, broccoli has extensive research behind it and found to be highly nutritious and disease fighting. For example, broccoli has sulforaphane, which is a well known anticancer compound. Other valuable contents of broccoli include amino acids, organic acids, sugars, glucosinolates, carotenoids, chlorophylls, vitamins E and K, essential mineral elements, and antioxidants.

Growing broccoli. Photo by Ch P.

Broccoli is part of the brassica group, also known as cruciferous, leafy vegetables that also includes cabbages and cauliflower. Similar to other brassicas, broccoli is separated into groupings when you harvest it. This means mostly two groups: a fall harvest crop and an early spring harvest crop. For a fall harvest, sow seeds in June or July or transplant from July to September. For an early spring harvest, sow seeds indoors starting in January or transplant from January to March. Broccoli is subject to bolting if it gets too warm, and this is usually a poor timing problem.

Broccoli thrives in humus-rich soil with plenty of mulch. They will grow up to two feet (ca. 0.6 m) tall and spread out a bit, so give them plenty of room. Full sun is needed for broccoli. It is best to plant at least 18 inches (ca. 0.5 m) apart. You can plant transplants a little deeper than they are growing in their pots. A top dressing of compost around them is recommended. Before the plant flowers, you can harvest the heads just about where the stem attaches and then wait for more florets to grow and harvest those. You can eat the stem and leaves as well.

As should be done with all brassicas, make sure to avoid growing them in the same location for consecutive years to avoid disease difficulties. Broccoli is not without pests and diseases. The most common pests for me are aphids, which get under the leaves, particularly during moist weather. You will notice the leaves sort of curling. The best way to deal with aphids, in my opinion, is with insecticidal soap. You will need to be persistent with your application of insecticidal soap, or the aphids will win the battle. Broccoli is also prone to similar pests as cabbage: caterpillars, snails, slugs, etc. *Bacillus thuringiensis* (BT) is a good organic tool for treatment of caterpillars and leaf-eating larvae.

Broccoli consists of types that produce one giant head (floret) or types that produce multiple florets. Romanesco varieties grow spirals of little florets. Good broccoli types for home gardens include early-spring-ripening Gypsy, which is bolt resistant, and fall-ripening Green Comet, Green Goliath, or Packman.

CABBAGE

Cabbage is another brassica that forms large edible heads of dense leaves. Cabbage is surprisingly versatile, as it is used around the world to make salad, coleslaw, kimchi, sauerkraut, and many other dishes. It can also be sautéed and braised. My family uses cabbage in soups and summer salad dishes.

Cabbage takes up a lot of space in the garden. It often looks small in the garden when you harvest it and suddenly looks gigantic when you bring it into the kitchen. It can, in fact, get gigantic. The current world record for giant cabbage is 138 pounds (ca. 63 kg), set in Alaska. Mature cabbage can be several feet across. They are generally easy to grow in well-conditioned soil. If you time it correctly, you could have cabbage year round. However, cabbage is not as popular a vegetable for some families. Because of this, I say three to six cabbage plants per year are plenty for a family of four. Any more than that, and you will likely get tired of it!

Green cabbage. Photo by Dan Cristian Paduret.

Cabbage is set into two different types based on the season in which it is harvested: early season and late season. In coastal environments, it is possible to grow cabbage year round due to the moderate temperatures; however, when inland, it is best to grow it at specific times. I plant cabbage in the January to March timeframe for an early spring harvest and in the July to September timeframe for a late-fall harvest. They need to be planted at least two feet (ca. 0.6 m) apart and in rows at least one foot (ca. 0.3 m) apart. Believe me, they will fill that space fast. When cabbage first starts growing in my garden, they almost always get cabbage caterpillars. You'll notice small holes developing, and then when you turn over the leaves, you will see little green worms that match the color of the leaf, chomping away. I consider it routine to spray *Bacillus thuringiensis* (BT, for short) on my cabbage plants as soon as I put them in the ground. After ingesting the BT, cabbage worms will immediately stop feeding. BT is considered an organic form of pest control and my preferred choice. Sevin® is also an effective pesticide that works for cabbage; however, it is not organic. This can come in powder or liquid form. You may also end up getting lots of slugs. They will eat the leaves of the plant and hide between them. I try to remove these by hand, avoiding the use of chemicals. It is best to remove the slugs at night when they are actively feeding. I must admit I will let them eat away at the outer leaves of the cabbage a bit. It is unsightly, but it doesn't seem to harm the plant much. Birds can wreak havoc early when you just plant your cabbage, particularly if you are growing them from seed and they start off small. Birds will kill your cabbage plant in one afternoon. Thus, my first choice is the transplant with bird netting.

For my early spring harvest, I plant Copenhagen or Red Jewel any time between January and March. Copenhagen grows fast and produces huge heads. The red cabbage types typically grow about half as fast in my garden. The heads don't get as large, either. You can plant Savvy or Ruby cabbage for a late-fall harvest. Chinese cabbage is also enjoyable to grow. This cabbage forms large, oblong heads that taste like a cross between lettuce and regular cabbage. These grow rapidly, and they are best planted in late summer. Chinese cabbage is finicky about the weather, and they won't produce heads if it is too cold. The best way to avoid that is to plant in late summer. Chinese cabbage is also loved by birds and is very prone to damage. Take precautions or your cabbage will be quickly destroyed.

***

CAULIFLOWER

Cauliflower is a brassica, and is a highly modified form of cabbage. It is a man-made vegetable developed by crossbreeding. The part of the plant you eat is a partially developed flower and its parts. However, cauliflower is high in vitamins B and C, has lots of fiber, and is high in antioxidants and phytonutrients that prevent cancer. Similar to other cruciferous vegetables, it is a good choice for health. Cauliflower can be steamed or roasted as a side dish, baked in a cheese sauce, added to rice dishes, or used as a main ingredient in curry. Cauliflower is similar to broccoli, except in color and has a milder taste.

Cauliflower is the most demanding of the brassicas to grow. It is more sensitive to heat and cold, and more challenging as a result. The key is good timing, adequate soil fertility, and good irrigation methods. Lots of sun is important unless it is really hot, in which case some shade is helpful. They need lots of room to grow, and I recommend at least 18 inches (ca. 0.5 m) in all directions. Cauliflower are heavy feeders, and a spray of fish emulsion every few weeks is very helpful. You can sow seeds indoors one month prior to the frost-free date or transplant for spring or early varieties. Cauliflower is frost tolerant; however, they won't thrive in cold weather. You can use row covers for extra help if needed. For the fall harvest, you can sow seeds indoors or outdoors after the last frost date.

The curd on a cauliflower is the part that you typically eat. Remember, I said cauliflower was more work? Well, the curd needs to be out of the sun. This will keep the curd white and help produce the best flavor. The way to do this is to tie the leaves together over the curd. You just take some string and pull the leaves up, tying them together. The term for this is blanching. This should be done when the curd is about two inches (ca. 5 cm) in diameter. You then harvest the heads when they're at least four inches (ca. 10 cm) across.

Cauliflower. Photo by Bikash Panda.

As should be done with all brassicas, make sure to avoid growing them in the same location for consecutive years to avoid disease problems. Cauliflower suffers from the same ills as other brassicas. The most common pests for me are aphids, which get under the leaves during moist weather. Look for telltale signs of aphids such as curling leaves. The best way to deal with aphids is with the persistent application of insecticidal soap. Cauliflower is also prone to similar pests as cabbage caterpillars, snails, slugs, etc. *Bacillus thuringiensis* is a good tool for caterpillars and leaf-eating larvae.

There are different colors of cauliflower, making them a lot of fun to grow and eat. White varieties such as Snowball and Snow King are common. The purple variety called Graffiti Hybrid is also popular, as is the orange variety called Cheddar Hybrid. The Cheddar Hybrid grows large orange cheddar-looking curds. For purple and orange, you don't need to blanch!

***

CHERRY

When George Washington was six years old, he received a hatchet as a gift. He then proceeded to go hack at a cherry tree on the family estate. When he confessed this to his father, his father was so pleased that he said that George's confession was worth more than 1,000 cherry trees. What a great story, huh? I know, it is not exactly appropriate to give a six year old kid a hatchet. It is thought to be a myth, but it is such a great story and involves a cherry tree, so I like it. Mt. Vernon had apples, pears, cherries, peaches, and apricots on the estate. It is a fascinating visit for a gardener and highly recommended.

In my opinion, cherries are difficult. I live in an area surrounded by cherry orchards, and every year is always this tense time when it is either too wet, too cold, or even too hot. It appears to be really difficult to please a cherry orchardist. I have found cherries to be difficult in my backyard, as well. One year, I can have an abundance of cherries, and the next year, I hardly have any. I can't explain it. It is like the tree takes every other year off. The other thing is that birds and animals absolutely love cherries, and you will need to do some things to protect this fruit. Of course, they're worth it. Cherries are the most delicious things, and they are nutritious as well. Who can pass up the cherry pie? Or just fresh cherries? Cherries also do best when they are accompanied by other cherry trees, and they must be compatible, or pollination will be weak or even nonexistent. They also need a good number of chill hours to be successful. Bings and Rainiers require 700 chill hours for successful production.

You guessed it. Cherries need full sun, and they need well-drained soil. Of course, rootstock can make a difference. Cherries, in general, don't handle dry soil well. Mulches are a great addition to a cherry orchard, as they have shallow root systems. Cherry trees don't need a lot of fertilizer, and they grow just fine without it. If you do notice your trees are not growing more than a foot a year, then definitely fertilize them. I have never had such a problem. My cherries easily grow three to five feet a year. They are vigorous plants.

Cherries have unique pruning needs. Because they are susceptible to bacterial problems, they should not be pruned during the dormant season. It is best to prune during the late summer while there's still enough growing time left and still enough time for wounds to heal quickly. I often watch to see when cherries are pruned in local orchards, and then I immediately get to my house and prune mine! The best way to get your cherry trees to produce a lot is to create several branches in a vase-like pattern. You cut out the central leader and allow a vase-like shape. Cherries will grow on wood between two and 10 years old. The best fruit is grown off of one to three-year-old wood. You will need to trim your cherries every year and prune them down considerably during the late summer. Cut off several feet, at least. Of course, it is okay to cut out damaged, diseased, and problem branches at any time of the year.

So, let's talk about large pests. I don't really spray my cherry trees other than with organic horticultural oil. Unless I have specific issues, no spray is needed. But pest protection is a must in my case. Birds will find my cherries from miles away. I only have four cherry trees in my backyard, and the pest pressure from birds is impressive. As the cherries get ripe, I install netting over the trees. I try to net them right before harvest time, before the bird pressure is awful, and keep the nets on the trees for the shortest time possible. If I do it too early, branches will grow through the netting,

Cherries. Photo by Lex Melony.

and it becomes nothing but a headache to remove. I throw the netting over the top and then pull it together at the trunk. You should have no areas where birds can squeeze through because they will try. The other thing that is very problematic for me is raccoons. Raccoons will climb up the tree at night, devouring all the cherries. Once they learn where your trees are, they will come back every year! I recommend placing reflective foil on the trunk and branches of the tree if raccoons are potentially a problem. They will also climb up netting and actually sit on top of the tree, chewing on the net and eating cherries through it. If it's a young tree and you can cover it completely with a net. Perhaps one of the best deterrents is to grow a tree with a tall trunk. This prevents the raccoons from climbing up. Combined with netting, this can at least slow them down. So those are the two most difficult pests that I have: birds and raccoons.

My absolute favorite cherry is the Rainier. Oh, boy, do I love Rainiers. My Rainier is a vigorous grower but, unfortunately, not a heavy producer. Of course, I also have a Bing cherry. Who could not have a Bing? These are great producers with fantastic-tasting cherries. Another one I have is a Lapins cherry. This is a very productive tree that produces cherries similar to Bing. Last, I have one very difficult named cherry. It is a Dave Wilson Bada Bing Ez-pick Cherry. I know it is a mouthful. These cherries are large and juicy. All these cherries require approximately 700 hours of chilling.

***

CITRUS

Who doesn't have a lemon tree in their backyard? Citrus trees are a beautiful part of the backyard as they are always bright green and lush looking plants, bearing fruit several months of the year. One does not need to live in a region with chill hours for citrus. Aside from their ornamental benefits, they offer an exceptional source of vitamin C, fiber, and folic acid.

Many know of the story of scurvy and how it was prevalent on long seagoing voyages in the 15th and 16th centuries, often killing more sailors than battles and shipwrecks alone. For hundreds of years, it was not understood what caused the dreadful disease of scurvy. Victims would get bleeding gums, ulcers, extremely low energy, and eventually die. James Lind, a Royal Navy surgeon's mate, actually ran a controlled experiment in 1747 that administered two oranges and one lemon a day to sailors, among other things, high in vitamin C. In less than a week, those who were eating oranges and lemons improved. This led to the cause of scurvy as some sort of vitamin deficiency. It was thought that citrus was one of the best treatments. Soon, lemon, lime, and orange juice or the entire fruit along with vegetables were required consumption on voyages, resulting in dramatically improved scurvy rates. Now, of course, we know that scurvy is the result of a vitamin C deficiency. Since we can't produce our own vitamin C, we need to acquire it from our foods. Citrus is very high in vitamin C. Scurvy is still prevalent today, mostly due to malnutrition. Citruses are indeed very important.

Lemon ready for harvest.

Common citrus grown in backyards today include orange, lemon, lime, grapefruit, kumquat, and tangerine citrus. Citrus trees are very popular in subtropical and tropical areas. Plenty of citrus also grow in Mediterranean-like climates, where temperatures will get as low as the 20s during the winter months. Citrus comes in standard or dwarf sizes. Dwarfs do well in containers, and standard-sized trees can reach 30 feet (ca. 9 m) if uncontrolled. If they are kept small, they can be protected with frost blankets as needed. They need full sun and like water one to two times a week. Typically, twice a week when they're young and once a week when they are older. Citrus trees need fast-draining soil, as overwatering can harm these trees. They are self fertile, often drawing significant numbers of bees at the flowering stage. Pruning should be done in the spring after the danger of frost has passed. You can prune them for shape, although it's not required for fruit. Citruses are usually grafted on top of vigorous rootstock. Make sure to remove sprouts coming from the trunk, particularly those that leave the trunk below the graft.

My staple is the Washington navel orange. The Washington navel orange is a common commercial orange tree. It is hardy and heavy bearing, doing well in hot interior valley regions. It ripens between

December and February and has large, sweet oranges that are easy to peel. The Meyer lemon on dwarf stock is an excellent choice for containers. These lemons are juicy and low in acidity, with thin skins. Mandarins are a fun citrus tree to grow, as the fruit provides nice decoration in the yard around the holidays. Of course, the flavor is unique. Limes, grapefruits, pomelos, and kumquats can be easily obtained.

***

CUCUMBERS

"We remember the fish we ate in Egypt that cost nothing—the cucumbers, the melons, the leeks, the onions, and the garlic. But now our strength is dried up, and there is nothing at all but this manna to look at." Numbers 11:5, the Bible (NIV version). This was written more than 3,000 years ago, in route from Mount Sinai to Canaan. So, we know that cucumbers were on the diet at least 3,000 years ago, probably a lot longer. The Greeks and Romans cultivated cucumbers; Charlemagne was said to grow them in Italy, and King Henry VIII ate them. Columbus is credited with taking cucumbers to the New World.

Today, these fruits are very popular in the garden. Despite what most think, they are fruit and not vegetables. They are popular around the world in salads, chilled soups, on sandwiches, as pickles, in water, sliced, on side dishes, etc. Cucumbers are very healthy. They are low in calories and packed with vitamins, minerals, and phytonutrients. For example, a half cup of cucumbers has six carbohydrates, three grams of protein, two grams of fiber, and 57% of the recommended daily value of vitamin K. Modest amounts of magnesium, potassium, and manganese also exist. One caution with store cucumbers is that they are often grown with pesticides; however, this isn't a problem if you are growing your own organically!

Cucumbers are aesthetic garden plants. They don't get super tall, are a nice green color, and they have pretty yellow blossoms. Cucumber plants can get fairly large, sprawling and spreading out over your garden, or growing up tomato cages. More compact varieties are also available. You don't need to plant a lot of cucumber plants for a family. In my opinion, three or four plants would be plenty for a family of four. They need warmth to germinate, grow, pollinate, and develop fruit. Since they're just summer plants, they need full sun, and, you guessed it, fertile, well-drained soil with lots of humus. You can plant your seeds one inch in the soil, either indoors or outdoors. Try to keep the soil evenly moist. Mulch is good for them, and try to get those cucumbers off the vine as soon as you see them at the right size. They get kind of gross when they're left on the vine for too long. They get seedy and tough.

Cucumber. Photo by Manmohan Pandey.

The best time to plant cucumbers directly in the soil is well after frost has passed. In my area, that is April, May, or even June. You can get cucumbers growing in as little as two months. Make sure you water them evenly as they are growing. We've all had that extra-bitter cucumber that is apparently caused by inconsistent watering. You can grow them in rows 18 inches (ca. 0.5 m) apart or on little hills approximately three feet (ca. 1 m) apart in your raised beds. I usually plant two or three plants going in different directions in the middle of a raised bed. I've had good luck planting them in rows and then directing the vines up into tomato cages. You can get a lot of vertical growth that way.

Whatever is sold as transplants or seeds distributed in your local area will drive a lot of what you see as choices. You can also order seeds online. I like lemon cucumbers. These are round, yellow, and sort of look like tennis balls when they're ripe. The plants are highly productive, and the skin is thin enough that I basically eat them raw from the garden like an apple. You need to pick them early enough so that the seeds don't get too big and they don't get too tough. I almost always overdo it with these and plant too many. You have probably seen the Armenian cucumber. It's not actually a cucumber, but a muskmelon, and it's commonly put in with the cucumbers at nurseries. Nevertheless, it tastes similar to a cucumber. These get quite large—eight inches (ca. 20 cm) to 10 inches (ca. 25 cm) or upwards of 24 inches (0.6 m) if you let them get too big. They are ribbed, pale green, highly productive, and worth growing. You can also grow pickling cucumbers easily. These have relatively thin skin. They can also be sliced and eaten that way. Some cucumbers have thick skin and need to be peeled.

***

GARLIC

Whenever I think of garlic, I think of the movie Lost Boys (Schumacher, 1987, 01:37). There was a scene when they were expecting a whole bunch of vampires at their house, and they were putting garlic in bathtubs, hanging it from banisters and doorways all over the house in an effort to repel the vampires. They must have hung hundreds of garlic cloves all over the house. The vampires showed up, and one of them said, "Garlic don't work, boys! It was a good try." Vampires aren't even real anyway, so I am not upset that garlic won't work for them. But garlic does have a rich and fascinating history of use, dating back more than 4,000 years. It was even used by the Egyptians and medieval Europe for curing everything from the black plague to heat stroke. Today, it continues to be touted as a heart healthy and cholesterol-lowering food. It is serious stuff. We use it in our kitchen more than I realize. It's easy to store and it comes in a nice, neat package (a bulb) that you can keep on the counter. You pull it apart and use separate cloves for cooking. It adds such a valuable flavor to some dishes that I will flat out refuse to cook the dish if we are out of garlic. More reasons to plant your own.

In the Mediterranean climate where I am, the best time to plant garlic is in the fall or early winter, usually about a month after onions. Technically, you can start planting them in September all the way through December; however, I find November or December to be the best time as the garden has been cleared from summer and is ready. They don't need a bunch of space. I find that 20 to 40 plants will supply a whole year's worth of garlic for my family of four. You get about six to twelve cloves of garlic in a bulb, depending on the type. The size of bulbs varies, and I strive to

Young garlic plants.

purchase at least one pound (ca. 0.5 kg) of garlic for planting purposes. Any more than two pounds (ca. 1 kg), I find, is too much.

Garlic bulbs are generally inexpensive and easy to ship; thus, you can purchase them at your local nursery or order your own online. Garden supply stores will sell garlic, usually along with bulbs. In my area, one must drive a good distance to find garlic bulbs for planting, and I commonly purchase my bulbs on Amazon or at my favorite online garden retailer. It is also possible to plant garlic you purchased from the grocery store; however, you must ensure it has not been sprayed or treated with chemicals that prevent it from growing. One note about elephant garlic: You will often find this type at garden stores and may be tempted to plant it. They are not true garlic but leeks. I have had some success with the elephant variety; however, they taste like mild garlic and take up a lot of space. Just a warning.

There are two basic types of garlic: hardneck and softneck. Hardneck or ophio garlic produces a stalk called a scape that grows through the center of the bulb. Hardnecks are very tasty but don't store as long as softnecks. Softneck garlic typically grows more cloves than hardnecks and does not send up a flower stalk or scape. They store longer than hardnecks. Most often, I will plant hardneck garlic, as they do best in fall planting. I am fond of Spanish Roja, Siberian, and Italian varieties.

What I do is prepare rows similar to my onion planting technique, making them about 12 inches (ca. 30 cm) apart and approximately six inches (ca. 15 cm) high. I would recommend amending your soil with manure and compost before planting. I then plant the garlic between four inches (ca. 10 cm) and six inches (ca. 15 cm) apart on the tops of the rows, burying the garlic about one inch (ca. 2.5 cm) below the top of the soil. If I don't plant the cloves deep enough, the roots will tend to push the clove out of the soil. Once planted, I cover them with several inches of mulch. I don't water them after planting and let the rain do its thing. If there is no rain for a while, I will start to give them a splash of water. They will handle the rain well; if it doesn't rain at all, you might want to give them a bit of water.

Approximately one month after planting your garlic, you will notice green, leafy-looking things popping out of the soil. These aren't true leaves but are called fronds. These are the beginnings of your garlic plant, as these two fronds will convert energy from the sun to your garlic plant. They are tremendously hearty and will survive the coldest of weather. There is not a lot of care needed over the next several months. The plants grow upright, with a main stem and leaves that grow laterally. Make sure the soil is moist but not too wet. You can put organic fertilizer on the soil during this time; however, I don't find this necessary. When the weather warms up and the plants appear to be maturing, hardnecks will develop a scape. The scape is a round-looking shoot that grows directly upwards. It actually has a little loop in it. It is recommended to cut the scape off when you notice it, as your garlic bulb will not develop as well with the scape. Scapes can be eaten, and there are many recipes available.

Your garlic will be ready for harvest in five to six months, which puts it in April or May. Once you notice the leaves of your garlic starting to turn brown at the tips, you know you are close. You can actually harvest the garlic early and eat it fresh. However, to make sure the bulbs are fully developed, wait until at least half of the leaves are brown. It is best to hold off on the water when you see the leaves starting to turn brown to prevent mold. It's easiest to harvest with a garden fork. I put the fork right underneath them and push up the soil, and up comes the garlic.

I dry my garlic by tying a bunch together and hanging them to dry in a warm location. Usually, this is the garden shed or garage. It takes several weeks to dry out. Once this happens, I cut them off just above the bulb and trim the roots. They are ready to give away, eat, or store.

***

GRAPES

"In the souls of the people, the grapes of wrath are filling and growing heavy, growing heavy for the vintage." John Steinbeck, Grapes of Wrath. Steinbeck describes the wonderful bounty of produce in California, luring people to the state from the eroding Great Plains during the Dust Bowl. The grape represented the great promise people sought. People were enticed by California, hearing rumors of high wages and an abundance of jobs. Instead, families were met with little work, low wages, and union problems, resulting in a very hard life. The promise of the grape was a failure, and in fact, it produced an unending wrath among migrants. Fortunately, the backyard grower today doesn't have to worry about wages or unions. You are in control!

Grapes are thought to have been around since humans. Evidence of wine was found in ceramic casks in Eurasia 8,000 years ago. It is thought that grapes were primarily used for wine around the world; however, they were also used in the Far East as a medicine, a social beverage, and a valuable commodity. Clean water was difficult to obtain, and wine was considered a healthy beverage to aid digestion. The wine market changed when it became known that Mediterranean grapes produced better-quality wine. When the Roman Empire fell during the first century, monasteries used wine as a religious rite, and wine continued to flourish as a social beverage as well. Other uses of grapes at the time included dried (raisins) and fresh table grapes.

Wine grapes.

The wine was brought to the New World by the explorers. The first wine in the New World was made in Jamestown in 1608 with native grapes. Early attempts to grow European grapes in North America failed due to pest problems and the fact that European varieties are not good at handling cold temperatures. Today, there are basically three types of grapes: American varieties, European varieties, and American and European hybrids. Production of European grapes in the United States is mostly in regions with mild winters, long growing seasons, and summers that are fairly dry with low relative humidity. American varieties generally handle the cold a little better. There are now more than 250 official varieties of wine-producing grapes in the United States.

Along the West Coast, our missionary friend Junipero Serra established the first vineyard and winery in California in 1769. Then, the Gold Rush came to California, and grapes were planted in the foothills for wine. Soon, cuttings were brought from Europe, and grapes were grown in their favored soil and climate throughout the West. Did you know that Washington, Oregon, and California make up more than 90 percent of all wine production in the United States? Each of these three states grows a unique set of varieties and offer countless wine varieties. California is the biggest producer of wine grapes by far.

I would be remiss if I didn't talk about the grapes of my hometown, Lodi, California. Lodi is unique in that it has a wonderfully productive soil called Tokay sandy loam and a dry Mediterranean climate with mild seasonal temperatures. The Lodi area started getting into grapes in the mid-1800s, first with Flame Tokay grapes. By the late-1890s, the two most common grapes in the Lodi area were Tokay and Zinfandel, although many European varieties were arriving frequently. Lodi is considered the Zinfandel capital of the world because it produces about 40 percent of the premium Zinfandel in California. Surprisingly, only about 25% of the grapes are currently Zinfandel, as there are now well over 100 varieties of grapes in Lodi.

It appears easy to start a variety of grapes of your choice by planting cuttings. Across the street from my home is a Tokay grape vineyard that is more than 100 years old. On the other side of our house is a German winery with dozens of varieties of German wine. Next to the German winery is a Spanish winery! Talk to the owners of these wineries, and they will tell you stories of growers planting cuttings brought from Europe.

Of course, grapes are not just used for wine. They are also eaten fresh, juiced and when not fermented, made into jellies and jams, dried as raisins, and even made into ointments and sprays. Come to the annual Lodi Grape Festival to see truck-sized murals of grapes! The sight of a grapevine with deep purple grape clusters among the bright green leaves is spectacular. In the yard, they can be used as border plants, espaliers, arbors, and focal plants.

Grapes are relatively easy to grow. They don't like wet feet, and it is recommended to plant them in raised beds if you have poor drainage. Grapes need full sun and need trellising. There are a variety of rootstock types for certain circumstances, such as disease resistance or particular pests, such as nematodes. The two types of backyard planting are basically wine grapes and table grapes. Some grapes can be used in many ways; however, most American varieties are used for table grapes, raisins, jams, and jellies, and European varieties are used for wine.

Grapes are seasonal plants like other fruit trees and grow quickly during the spring and summer. Dormancy occurs over the winter months, and grapes thrive on winter chill. They are pruned during dormant periods and partially pruned again during the summer for various reasons. Grapes are typically self pollinated as they have both male and female grapes on one plant. The best time to plant grapes is in January or February. Once planted, irrigate. No more irrigation will be needed until there is approximately one foot of growth during the spring. Grapes typically ripen during the fall, and each variety has its own specific ripening dates.

There are a few common pests and diseases that backyard growers need to watch for. The biggest is powdery mildew, which will cause the developing grapes to shrivel and fail to ripen. This is treated with sulfur powder. Other pests include insects such as leafhoppers, spider mites, and thrips. There are many organic choices for controlling these pests, and if things get out of control, there are always non-organic controls.

A very popular grape for juice, jams, and raw eating is Concord grapes, which are a native of North America that produces small, dark purple grapes that get insanely sweet when they ripen in September. These are definitely seeded grapes, as you get a mouth full of seeds with a mouth full of sweetness when you eat them. Other popular table grapes include Thompson Seedless, Tokay, and Red Globe. There are many varieties of wine grape plants available; however, the most popular include Cabernet Sauvignon, Zinfandel, Riesling, Gewürztraminer, Blanc, and Chardonnay.

***

HERBS

What an interesting history herbs have! Unlike any other plant, herbs have been used by humans for a very long time. For example, they have found herbs depicted on cave paintings in France that were dated between 13,000 and 25,000 BC. Historically, herbs were not just used for food but also for medicine, air fresheners, ointments, and the treatment of an assortment of health maladies. The ancient Egyptians used herbs to embalm for burial. Herbs played a huge role medically before hospitals and the development of modern medicine. The 20th century saw a drop in the use of herbs for medical purposes; however, they still exist in the herbal homeopathic health sector and are used by many in the kitchen.

Herbs are defined as a plant used for medicinal purposes, as a flavor for food, or as a scent. Herbs are unlike vegetables in that they have a variety of life cycles and can be grown in consecutive years or just once, depending on the type. They can be classified based on their life cycle. Annual herbs such as basil are only grown in one season in most cases. An annual plant is a plant that completes its life cycle within one growing season. That means everything from germination to the production of seeds. Perennial herbs grow and bloom over the spring and summer, die back in the fall and winter, and then return in the spring. A less common category of herbs is the biennial. These herbs take two years to complete their life cycle in Mediterranean climates. Because many of these will grow beyond two years, they are treated as perennials. It is helpful to understand which type of herb you have in order to grow it in your backyard. Perennial herbs do well along the edges of beds and in visible locations, and annuals can be planted in rows in beds where regular cultivation is easy. You can also group them together based on their sunlight requirements. Herbs are a large lot containing upwards of 3,000 types, and seeds of many can be purchased. Or the more common herbs can be acquired as transplants.

Herbs do well in rich soil, well-draining pots, or raised beds. You don't need a bunch of them for culinary purposes, mostly just one plant of each type, as the leaves and parts of a plant go a long way in the kitchen. You can make herb gardens out of different colors and shapes of leaves in pots or raised beds. Of course, you can dry many herbs to make potpourri or tea. In my opinion, I don't get enough out of my herbs. I plant basil and several types of herbs during the summer months, and we use them sparingly in the kitchen, but I really just don't focus on them as they seem to be overshadowed by the fruits and vegetables. There is much to be tapped here. You need to plant your herbs after all the danger of frost has passed. Either start them from seed or transplant small plants. Because herbs come in a variety of types, I will address some of the more popular ones below.

Basil

Basil is an annual herb that does best in sunny locations. I find basil to be very useful in the kitchen. It is a major player in Italian dishes and has such a great scent. We often just cut it and put it in the water in the kitchen. It stays fresh for weeks and smells so pleasant. It is easy to grow, with the exception that it really doesn't like frost. Also, you need to pinch the tips to create a bushy plant, or it will get tall and woody. If it starts to flower, you can also cut those tips off, and it'll get bushy. It is easy to give bunches of basil away to friends by putting a little water in a bag with the cuttings. Most people love basil gifts. Making pesto with it is a very common culinary desire. Basil is also a good companion plant with peppers, tomatoes, and several other types of plants. I try to plant basil between my tomato plants.

Basil.

Parsley

Parsley is an annual herb that likes a little shade. Several parsley varieties are available, and they are all equally easy to grow. These, of course, are a key flavor in many types of dishes. Parsley can be puréed into sauces and pesto and is often added to dishes like pasta, sauces, salads, meat dishes, and vegetables. Parsley is frequently sprinkled on the top of finished dishes for appearance and herbal flavor. Did you know parsley can give you lots of energy? It is a common juicing ingredient and gives you long-lasting energy. You must pick parsley frequently to keep your supply of fresh leaves. You can keep parsley growing in the colder months by keeping it covered.

Mint

Mint is a perennial that will grow and spread quickly. It is classified as invasive, and if given plenty of water and partial sun, it will spread rapidly. Mint leaves are a great addition to water or tea, potato dishes, or certain types of meat, such as roast lamb. I grow mint next to our house, and it provides a nice scent, particularly when I am cutting it back!

Rosemary

Rosemary is a perineal that can handle lots of sun and heat. However, it needs well-drained soil. Once established, rosemary is fairly drought tolerant. They are fast growers and will get several feet tall unless you prune them regularly. Rosemary adds flavor to a variety of meat dishes, such as lamb, pork, and veal. It will also add a great aroma to your garden. Although there is no scientific evidence, rosemary is often used for memory, indigestion, fatigue, hair loss, and many other purposes.

Sage

Sage is a slow-growing perineal. Because sage has a unique look, I highly recommend planting it in an herb garden if you are seeking it for aesthetic purposes. Sage has green-grayish leaves, adding a lot of structural variety to your plot. But sage also has dietary benefits. It is packed with antioxidants and vitamins and is thought to be healthy for you. You can use sage in chicken dishes, soups, even in a chicken pot pie, and with sausage and other things of that nature.

Oregano

Oregano is a perennial with small, circular, and aromatic leaves, making it a great addition to the garden. Oregano seasons Mediterranean foods and you can even get varieties that suit your favorites, such as Greek or Italian varieties. Some oregano varieties are more decorative than culinary, and they can be bland, so check before planting if you are interested in using them for culinary purposes. I once had an oregano plant that had no flavor whatsoever. It had beautiful green leaves and was fast growing.

Thyme

Thyme is a perennial and compact plant with cute, small leaves that can be used year round. It's a great complement to an herb garden and great in the kitchen. It goes well with other Mediterranean herbs, such as oregano, and is widely used in cooking. Thyme can be added to potatoes, rice, and vegetables, for example. Ancient Egyptians used thyme in their embalming practices, and ancient Greeks used it as incense. Thyme is also touted, though not scientifically proven, to help with fighting acne, lowering blood pressure, and helping to alleviate coughs.

Tarragon

There are different types of tarragon, and French is the primary one used in the kitchen. French tarragon is the commonly grown temperate-zone tarragon used for culinary purposes. Tarragon has a sweet anise flavor. You can clip the leaves into salads and on top of soups or flavor sauces, as well as add them to shellfish, fish, chicken, and turkey meals.

***

INTERSPECIFIC FRUIT TREES

There are a dizzying number of interspecific fruit trees. These are two or more fruits crossed to make a unique fruit. Some of these crosses have been around for several hundred years, and some have only recently been developed. Often, when these fruits are crossed, the best part of each is combined into one fruit, and they can be spectacular. I will do my best to summarize the major categories, and I encourage the reader to further investigate interspecifics. Because I am a fan of Dave Wilson Nursery and their affiliation with a California fruit breeder named Floyd Zaiger of Zaiger Genetics, many of the interspecifics mentioned below are Zaiger Genetics hybrids.

Like most fruit trees, interspecifics need at least six hours of sun and well-drained soil. They don't like to sit in saturated soil. Prune for structure during the dormant season, removing branches that clog up the center of the tree. Summer pruning is helpful to keep the trees at a manageable size.

The pests associated with these types of trees are no different than those associated with plums, apricots, and nectarines. Birds will find them quickly when they ripen, and other wildlife will devour them if allowed. Watch carefully and take the customary precautions.

Pluot®

The Pluot® is one of the most popular interspecifics. These fruits are relatively new to the scene, and they are making a bang! Pluots® were developed in 1989 by Zaiger Genetics. The Pluot® is a cross between a plum and an apricot. More specifically, it is 75% plum and 25% apricot. Pluot® trees appear to have the vigor of plum trees and contain fruit that is a delicious combination of the flavors of plum and apricot. The nice thing about most Pluot® varieties is that they don't have the bitter skin like plums do, yet they have the intense sweetness of plums and apricots. There are more than 80 varieties of Pluots® today, and California leads the production of them. Pluots® are quite nutritious, being low in calories and a good source of vitamins A and C, fiber, and potassium. These trees are pretty easy to take care of, as they are vigorous. I find Pluots® are best eaten fresh, right off the tree; however, they can be used similarly to plums. There are many colors and flavors to choose from.

I currently have six varieties of Pluots® growing in my backyard orchard, including the Dapple Dandy, Flavor Supreme, Flavor Grenade, Splash, Emerald Drop, and Geo Pride. Note that four of these varieties are on a four-way tree, and each main branch provides a different variety. They each have a unique color and ripen at different times between mid-July and late September. Chill hour requirements range between 400 and 800 hours.

Aprium®

Cotton candy Aprium®.

The Aprium® is another Zaiger Genetics special. This is a cross between an apricot and a plum, that consists of 75% apricot and 25% plum. The Aprium® fruit resembles an apricot in texture and size; however, these interspecifics include the most amazing flavor. My favorite is the Cot-N-Candy Aprium®. This variety is technically a white Aprium® and ripens in mid- to late June and only requires approximately 400 hours of chill. It is also self fruitful. The fruit is so sweet that it resembles cotton candy, and there is little bitterness associated with the skin. In addition, no fuzz on the skin. If I could only grow one fruit tree, this would be it! There aren't as many varieties of Aprium® as Pluots®; however, there are still plenty to choose from in the event you can't comprehend a fruit that tasks like cotton candy!

NectaPlum® and Peacotum®

The NectaPlum® is a Zaiger Genetics cross between a nectarine and plum, with mostly nectarine. There is currently only one type of NectaPlum® called Spice Zee. The Spice Zee requires only 200–300 chill hours and ripens from mid-July to August. The Spice Zee has flavors of nectarine and plum in one fruit. The Peacotum® is a Zaiger three-way cross between a peach, an apricot, and a plum. The only variety so far is the Bella Gold, which requires approximately 500 chill hours.

Other Interspecifics

Pleuerry™ is a Zaiger Genetics cross between a plum and a sweet cherry. A Plumcot is a 50:50 cross between a plum and an apricot, as opposed to Pluots®, which are 75:25. There is a cherry-plum interspecific and a peach-plum as well. More interspecifics are coming out all the time.

***

LETTUCE

Lettuce needs full sun but doesn't like the heat. It is basically a cool-season vegetable. Hot summer-like heat is not good for lettuce, as it makes it bitter. They like fertile, evenly moist soil that drains well. One thing that I have learned about lettuce is that it seems to be prone to pests. If you live in a location where there are rabbits, they will find your lettuce. Birds seem to really enjoy pecking at lettuce leaves and completely destroying them. I must cover my lettuce either with row covers or bird netting to prevent destruction by pests. This will prevent me from planting lettuce in many cases, as it's just too much of a headache. But know that it is definitely possible to grow lettuce, especially in the cooler months.

Leaf lettuce is the easiest type to grow. It matures quickly, and you can even harvest it leaf by leaf, a little bit at a time. You can keep those plants going for a long time by taking a few leaves from each plant for your salads. Romaine lettuce is upright and, in my opinion, the easiest lettuce to make a salad with. It's easy to cut and wash. They will mature in about 70 days. I would consider these mildly hard to grow. Finally, there is the crisp head lettuce. These are the most difficult to grow. We know of iceberg lettuce, which is this type. They have compact heads with crisp leaves. They need a long, cool season and constant attention. The slightest bit of stress, and the plants will prematurely bolt. I have never been so bold as to plant an iceberg of lettuce. Perhaps I will give it a shot sometime, as it would be a great challenge!

Lettuce. Photo by Erda Estremera.

You can plant lettuce by seed or transplant. Know that lettuce seeds are very heat sensitive. They don't last long in storage, and they are a little tricky to start. For a higher rate of success, one may want to use transplants. You can purchase lettuce transplants of many types at your local nursery. If you are planting by seed, it is important to get all the rocks and large dirt clods out of the soil. You need nice soil for your seeds. Plant the seeds a quarter inch below the surface and keep the ground moist. It will take up to 10 days for lettuce to germinate, and you will need to thin them to one plant every 12 inches (ca. 30 cm) or so once they are a few inches tall. The best time to sow lettuce is dependent on the type. Leaf lettuce is best sown in early spring or in the fall. Head lettuce should be sown in the winter or in the early fall. Lettuce is shallow rooted, and it requires frequent watering. A bit of nitrogen fertilizer helps tremendously.

There are more than a dozen common varieties of lettuce that one can plant in their backyard. I have had especially good luck with the Mesclun mix. Mesclun is a mix of tender salad greens and herbs. A Mesclun blend includes Arugula, Chervil, Oak Leaf, and Mâche. It can also be made of a combination of different greens, including Dandelion greens, Frisée, Endive, baby spinach, collard greens, mustard greens, Radicchio, kale, and more. If you sow a row up to five feet (ca. 1.5 m) long every few weeks, you can have fresh salad greens consistently when these plants are ready for harvest. Be sure to protect them from the birds, snails, and rabbits! Other salad greens that have been pretty simple for me to grow include Butter Crunch, Salad Bowl, Looseleaf, and Butter Head. Give lettuce a try, and hopefully, you'll have some success. If your family is like mine, you have a salad every night with your meal. It is the most crucial part of our meal and is the way that I get my healthy greens in!

MELONS

Hang out in the produce section of a store during melon season, and you will see people thumping the melons, smelling them, spinning them, and doing all sorts of funny things to determine ripeness. What joy melons bring! The melon group encompasses not only many types of melons, but technically, the melon group includes cucumbers, squash, and pumpkins! For the sake of this chapter, I am only going to cover the more traditional melons, such as watermelon, cantaloupe, muskmelon, Honeydew, and Crenshaw. Cucumbers, squash, and pumpkins will be covered separately. Melons are low in the bad things, such as sodium, saturated fat, and cholesterol, and high in the good things, such as fiber, vitamin K, potassium, copper, vitamin C, and vitamin B6. Who can forget that amazing and unique melon taste on a hot summer day? There are so many types of melons that it would be difficult to summarize all of them here. They can be as small as one pound to upwards of several hundred pounds. The current world record for watermelon is 350 pounds (ca. 159 kg)! Melons are very popular in my household. We anticipate the beginning of watermelon season every year, and we begin purchasing them as soon as we see them in stores. We try them as soon as they become available, critiquing their flavor and sweetness. Then finally, the peak of watermelon season comes, and the flavor is just unbelievable. We eat watermelon every night at dinner when they are in season. It is cut into pieces and kept cold in the refrigerator for snacking as well.

Melons are vine-like plants that are easy to grow and cultivate and are highly recommended for your garden if you have the space. Melons do well in fertile soil in hot sunny locations and are heat loving and sensitive to frost, so they should be planted after the danger of frost has passed. This is between March and June, similar to tomatoes and other fruits and vegetables. I often shy away from March, as there are still cold spells that frequently occur. I would say late April, May, or June would be ideal. You can start your own plants from seed indoors, sow them directly from seed in your garden, or purchase transplants. For those sowing the seeds, you can get specific planting depths and particulars on the seed packaging. They do need a lot of space, and I recommend planting them at least five feet (ca. 1.5 m) apart, so they have enough room. I am guilty of overcrowding them, and it still works. Just beware; it's going to be a big, tangled mess! If you overcrowd them, your yields will likely go down a bit. You will have harvestable fruit in approximately three months.

Watermelon hiding in the vines.

The great thing about growing your own melons is that the plants actually have telltale signs when they are ripe. First watermelon. Watermelon plants have a little tendril growing from the stem. It is a short, thin, spindly part of the plant. Sometimes, it can curl and resemble a pig's tail. This little tendril is your signal. It will start to turn brown when your watermelon is ripe. The ideal time to pick your watermelon is when that tendril is halfway brown. Believe me, this works. I have actually been impatient and tried to pick my watermelon early, thinking the tendril just wasn't doing its job, and sure enough, the fruit was not ripe enough. So be patient and wait for it to happen. As for cantaloupe-like melons, they have something called a slip. This refers to where the stem attaches to the fruit. If you push on the stem and it slips off the fruit, you have a full slip, and your melon is ripe. These methods are a great way to tell when you have ripe fruit when it is growing in your garden. Imagine if you were growing melons commercially and had to determine the best time to harvest them for shipment. Home gardeners definitely have an advantage in ensuring peak flavor and ripeness.

In my experience, all types of melons are easy to grow and taste exceptional when they come from the home garden. Watermelon is a blast. They get big and heavy, and you really feel like you've produced something significant. Melons are tremendously sweet and just go great in the kitchen. I am also a big fan of Ambrosia melons.

ONIONS

Onions are easy to grow, easy to store, and easy to use in the kitchen. That is very easy! Of course, there are many health benefits. After all, they are vegetables. You need to eat your vegetables! One thing about onions is that they do take a long time to get to a good harvestable size, and they will take up space in your garden for a long time. I plant them in November and tend to start harvesting them in May or June. If you're short on space, this can become annoying. When you are ready to put your tomatoes in the ground, you still have these onions taking up space.

Onions are classified by the number of hours of daylight required for the plant to grow bulbs—the part of the plant that is the onion. Short-day onions begin to develop bulbs when the day length increases to a length of 10 to 12 hours, and long-day onions require 14 to 16 hours of sunlight to grow bulbs. Of course, there are day neutral types too. Most onions grown in North America are long-day onions. If you are getting your onion supplies locally, this shouldn't be a problem, but beware if you are purchasing them online, as things will get all messed up if you grow the wrong type in your area. One more detail: there are different options to start your onions, and I have tried all of them. One way is to start them by seed. You plant seeds just underneath the top of loose soil in late summer. Another way is to plant sets, which basically look like miniature onions about the size of marbles. To plant these, you place them in the soil with the bulb at the surface. Transplants are my favorite approach. These are little onion plants that have been grown from seed at a nursery. Transplants are planted approximately one inch (ca. 2.5 cm) deep, and after a few weeks of adjusting, they will take off quickly. By far, my best success has come from transplants. It probably helps that one of the largest transplant suppliers in the state is two miles (ca. 3.2 km) from my house! Valley Transplants in Acampo, California, sells to farmers, nurseries, and even homeowners.

Young onion plants.

Onions are best planted in the fall in the Central Valley of California. Fall planting is an excellent time as pest pressure is low and temperatures are not typically hot, allowing for a low stress start. It goes without saying that you need adequate sunlight and nutrient-rich soil to grow onions. I don't think they are persnickety about soil, however. What I do is dedicate approximately two eight-foot (ca. 2.4 meter) x eight-foot (ca. 2.4 meter) raised garden beds each year. Make sure you rotate locations to avoid disease. It never hurts to fortify your soil with manure and compost before planting. I make rows and plant my onions on top of the rows, about four inches (ca. 10 cm) to six inches (ca. 15 cm) apart. Elevated rows are really helpful, as they will help you get through rainy periods by draining water from the roots, avoiding rot. I also use the rows to deep water the onions as they mature in the early summer.

To plant my transplants, I grab a handful of them and trim them off about six inches (ca. 15 cm) from the bottom, so they have fresh cuts. I plant them about half a finger deep in the soil. I use my finger to drive them in. The soil should be nice and soft at this point, and the roots should head down with my finger. I generally plant them about four inches (ca. 10 cm) apart. I probably plant them too closely. You could go six inches (ca. 15 cm) apart to give them more room. What I do is plant them fairly close and then harvest every other onion as they get larger. I also eat the greens in salads or as garnishes before some onion bulbs mature. You can harvest the greens almost anytime.

After I plant, I water them well, soaking the soil thoroughly. From here on, I make sure that the soil is always moist but not too wet. A week or two after planting, I apply an organic fertilizer. A month or two after that first fertilizer application, I fertilize again with organic fertilizer. During the first few months of the season, I just sprinkle the onions in the morning as long as it's not too warm, and I give them a good soaking about two to three days a week. However, once the roots get bigger and the onion bulbs develop, I will flood the rows to water them. When early summer comes, your onions will be impressively large—several feet high—with bright green leaves and bulbs quickly gaining in size at the base near the ground. One thing that can get annoying is bolting. This occurs when the onion plant starts to flower. It will send up a single round stem that develops a seed-bearing flower at the end. If you want to harvest seeds, this is one way to do it; however, the onion bulb will stop growing and lose flavor when this happens. Bolting onions should be harvested as soon as you see the bolting, and they should be eaten as soon as possible, as they don't save well. Some years, I get a little bolting. Maybe just a few. In other years, I get a handful of bolts. I think the weather has something to do with it. Also, my yellows and whites bolt more than my reds—another reason why I like reds.

A few things about pests: I have these annoying little birds that run all over the place during the fall time period, and they will destroy my onions if I don't cover them with netting. I use bird netting for the first month or two to get the onions off to a good start. Other pest problems I've had include gophers. Gophers will eat the roots and then start eating the onion. These pests can cause some serious damage, so the gophers must be controlled quickly. I avoid poison and catch my gophers with underground traps.

During early summer, you will notice the bulbs forming. You can start harvesting at any time. I like to wait until they are about baseball size. To harvest, I use a garden fork and drive the fork underneath the onions to loosen them and then pull them out. They are great to eat fresh, and it is also recommended if you want to store them for a longer amount of time to put them in the shade in a dry environment for several weeks. I will put them underneath my fruit trees in order for them to be shaded and breathe while they cure. After several weeks, the green leaves will die back, and you can pretty much just pull off the leaves that have now turned brown. I tend to cut the roots before I bring them to the house, as they will carry a lot of dirt with them. If cured properly, they will last for months. I will often have them sitting by the back door in the shade between June and October and just eat them as needed. I also save some by curing them, wrapping them individually in aluminum foil, and putting them in the refrigerator. They tend to last months in this situation. I've also cut them up and frozen them; however, I feel that freezing them is sort of difficult because they get watery. One year, I borrowed a dehydrator and dried a bunch of onions. These were kept for a very long time.

If you grow a lot of onions like me, you're going to have several hundred pounds of onions ready to be harvested in May or June. What I do is harvest 20 pounds (ca. 9 kg) or 30 pounds (ca. 14 kg) at a time and just put them on the back porch, and whenever someone comes to my house, they get some onions. Some people just absolutely love onions, and you can give a bunch to them. Others don't like them as much and you might need to hide them in the bags of tomatoes or other produce you give them. Be sure to share so that people think you're some sort of master at growing them. But really, they don't take much effort. They're super easy, but nobody needs to know that. You can also share your transplants because, after all, they're one or two cents each, so people think you're being really generous. but really, you're only sharing $0.25 worth of onions. One last thing: I love giving garden tours to kids. They have no idea what an onion looks like. Don't miss out on that!

My favorite type of onion to grow is the Red Burger. The Burger is an intermediate-day variety that takes 172 days to mature. I use these in everything from eggs to salads, burritos, and soup. They have a mild onion flavor and are also on the sweet side. I also commonly grow the yellow Merlin 1122 onion, the long-day torpedo onion (long and skinny), and even whites. When you purchase these from a supplier, they are extremely inexpensive; the price depends on the quantity you purchase. I commonly plant between 100 and 200 onion transplants a year. This will fill at least two of my garden beds.

PEARS

Pears are good for you. They are known to boost heart health, are anti-inflammatory, and promote good gut health, among other things. Compared to apples, pears are still second best, and far more apples are consumed than pears. Pears are separated into two types: European and Asian. The European pear is the one that we are most familiar with. These are picked before they are ripe and continue to ripen off the tree, making them of great commercial use. Asian pears are shaped more like an apple and are picked when they are ripe. They also have thick skin.

All pears will tolerate non-ideal soil conditions and do well in moist, cloudy weather. A good, thick mulch layer is always recommended for pears. They will grow rapidly, and fertilizing them is not necessary. Euro-

Warren pear.

pean pears take four to six years to start to bear fruit, while Asian pears take two to three years to bear fruit. Pruning is similar to apple trees and depends on choice. You can prune with a central leader for a few years and then cut it back or prune out the central leader early for a bush type of plant. Pears tend to grow very upright, and you may find it necessary to spread branches or weigh them down to increase the angle and spread of branches. You will also likely need to thin your pears to get full-sized fruit.

Fireblight is the most serious concern for pears. This disease affects all parts of the tree and can spread rapidly, killing your tree. One way to reduce the prevalence of this disease is to prune lightly, and you can also acquire fireblight-resistant varieties. I lost two pear trees during my first year of fruit tree growth to this nasty disease. Other diseases and pests I have yet to deal with include codling moth, canker, crown gall, leaf spot, and powdery mildew.

My Warren pear is fireblight resistant, self pollinating, and a superfast grower. It grows an excellent-flavored dessert pear of medium to large size. The Warren ripens in August and is the only pear I have or need.

***

PEACHES AND NECTARINES

Peaches and nectarines don't store well, and the ones you get in the stores usually taste terrible. Unless, for some miraculous reason, the stores get them ripe from orchards nearby during harvest season. Otherwise, they're unappetizing, and I never even buy them at stores. When they're growing on your trees, you can time the ripeness to perfection. There's nothing like a perfect peach or nectarine. To me, the trees are vigorous yet demanding. There's the peach leaf curl thing and the pruning requirements. Heavy pruning and pretty good pest pressure make these fruit trees pretty tough to handle but worth every bit. They have some average chill requirements. It's all worth it, as fresh peaches and nectarines are just fantastic. This fruit is usually so tasty that I don't even need to cook it or do anything. I just eat them fresh, like candy. Some years, when we have an abundance, peach cobbler or nectarine fruit salad is made.

Peaches and nectarines grow just fine in ordinary garden soil; however, these plants like dry, sandy soils. Heavy, wet soils are not preferred. Of course, the type of rootstock will determine the final soil preferences. These trees do grow quickly and, in most cases, do not need fertilizer. Have patience that first year. Once established, they will produce lots and lots of fruit. Peaches and nectarines are not as long lived as some other fruit trees, such as cherries and apples. Approximately 10 years is the lifespan of these trees.

Peaches. Photo by Jason Leung.

Pruning for structure can be done during the dormant season. Try to open the center of the plant for airflow and cut out damaged limbs and limbs growing in the wrong direction. Branches that are one to two years old should be preserved, as these are the most productive. Summer pruning after harvest is also a good option to limit the size of these fast-growing trees. Peaches and nectarines are so vigorous, they can handle very heavy pruning and will bounce back quickly. I often cut back approximately 30% of the size of these trees, sometimes as much as 50%. I have never had adverse effects from the heavy pruning of these trees.

Once you begin to get fruit, you need to make sure you thin your peaches and nectarines. These trees produce a lot of fruit, and if you don't do thinning, you will end up growing too many fruits, breaking branches, and having small fruit. There are a couple of ways you can do this. One way is to get a stick and just knock the heck out of your branches. Keep knocking until the density is right for you. A good time to do this is when they are small—about marble size or even smaller. Another way to thin is by hand, which is my preferred method. Although it takes a lot of time, I find it somewhat therapeutic, and I can be very specific about how many I want on each branch. Generally, I shoot for one peach or nectarine for every six inches (ca. 15 cm) or so. Of course, I remove anything that looks deformed or messed up. Large branches can handle more peaches; small branches can handle fewer. It's that simple.

Earwigs love peaches and nectarines, and it's a must to get control of these pests, as well as ants and other things that will crawl up the trunk of your tree. Tree Tanglefoot is an absolute lifesaver. I wrap a solid barrier of this sticky goop on nearly all of my tree trunks in early summer. This is a great organic insect control option. Leaf curl can get pretty bad during wet years, and I prevent this with a spray every year of horticultural oil and copper. Horticultural oil is considered an organic spray;

however, copper is not. I am sure to follow all label directions exactly. Of course, birds love to put their beaks in peaches and nectarines, usually the day before you are ready to pick them. They are really annoying. Once your peach trees get sufficiently sized, this typically isn't too big of a problem. I have enough peaches and nectarines to share with the birds. However, I will occasionally drop a bird net over the tops of my trees just to reduce the damage. I will also put some of that scare tape up in hopes of scaring birds off. There doesn't seem to be as much pressure on peaches and nectarines as there is on cherries. That's another story.

There are many varieties of peaches and nectarines to choose from, and I strive for varieties that ripen successively and are freestones. Freestone means the pit comes out easily. My absolute favorite peach is the July Elberta peach, also called the early Elberta. It produces lots of big, juicy peaches with wonderful flavor. It's self fruitful, which means that it doesn't need another tree to pollinate it, and it requires between 400 and 500 chill hours. When these beauties are ripe, I will eat several of them right off the tree while I am in the yard. I usually get peach juice all over my face. So, I just grab the hose and clean off my face! I also have the O'Henry peach. These are good-flavored peaches, and they come in a little after the July Elberta. Not quite as large and not quite as tasty, in my opinion, but they are still a very good peach. Another type of peach I have is the Saucy Swirl Saucer peach. These guys come early, and they're shaped like little saucers. They are freestone, and fun little tasty treats. They're one of the first fruits that come during the summer, and I always like to see them. As far as nectarines go, I have several types, although I don't think I have my favorite yet. I have the Snow Queen nectarine, which has a good flavor. It only needs 250 to 300 hours of chill, and it is self fruitful. These will be ready in late June. I also have a Honey Kist nectarine. This ripens early and requires about 500 chill hours. It is self fruitful and has worked reasonably well.

PEPPERS

Peppers are amazing. Just think about the power a pepper has. They spice up all types of dishes, create salsa, and can add heat to any meal. They can be sweet, mild, or super hot, causing blisters in your mouth. They can bring the strongest of men to their knees or even send them to the hospital. The same pepper that sends someone to the emergency room won't affect another with tolerance for the heat. They can be yellow, red, green, white, black, blue—you name it. Pepper plants are pleasant looking, reaching a height of two to three feet (ca. 0.6 to 0.9 m) in most cases, with dark green leaves and pretty-colored peppers. What a great bunch of colors to include in your vegetable garden! Peppers hold on to the plant for a long time, and you don't have to eat them right away like some types of fruit. They can hold on for weeks and weeks. Pick them when you want them.

Bell pepper. Photo by Greg Daines.

Pepper plants definitely need heat. If you're growing them from seeds, you can start them indoors one to two months prior to planting. They are slow starters, in my opinion, so give them plenty of time. I would not put them in the ground until May at the earliest. The soil needs to be nice and warm for these plants. If you put them in the ground when it is too cold, they're going to sit there and do nothing for at least a month if they make it. It still takes them a bit of time to get going, but once they get going, they produce lots and lots of peppers into November. They require well-conditioned soil and full sunlight. You can plant them 12 inches (ca. 30 cm) to 18 inches (ca. 46 cm) apart, and they also need to be staked. I usually put the stakes in at the same time I'm planting them, so I can install the stake next to the plant without disturbing the roots. As these plants grow and get peppers, they can get so heavy that the branches will break. You need stakes to keep that from happening and to protect them from the wind, which will also snap branches.

There are lots of peppers to choose from, and I will go over a few of the types that I grow in my yard. Of course, local supply, nurseries, and hardware stores will somewhat dictate the type of peppers that you come across. You can order just about any type of pepper seed online. I split peppers into two groups: sweet peppers and hot or spicy peppers. As far as sweet peppers go, my first choice to grow is Italian sweet peppers. Italian pepper plants can get fairly tall and are prolific. They will produce nice, sweet peppers up to 12 inches (ca. 30 cm) long with no bitterness. I chew on these constantly when I am working in the garden when they are ready. You can use them in any dish that calls for sweet peppers. My favorite dish to use these for is an unstuffed pepper recipe. These guys really need to be staked as they get tall, and they get really heavy with peppers. Pick them frequently and stake them early. The next sweet pepper I would recommend would be any type of bell pepper. It is easiest to grow green bell peppers, but you can grow just about any color. They have white, orange, red, yellow, purple, black, and everything in between. These don't get quite as tall as Italian peppers, but nothing beats a bell pepper. You can stuff them, chop them up and put them in salads and all types of dishes, and of course, you can eat them raw right off the plant! Other types of sweet peppers I enjoy are the multicolored sweet mini pepper and the Shishito pepper, which are little wrinkled-up peppers that are great in salads. Just cut them up, seeds and all, and put them in salads. They have interesting texture and are sort of chewy. The Shishito, in particular, is low growing and heavily bearing. There is no need to stake these plants. I would recommend six plants of sweet peppers for your garden to feed a family of four.

As far as spicy peppers go, I am not very brave. I will usually grow three or four different types, but about as spicy as I get is a Habanero. I think everyone should definitely grow at least one Jalapeño pepper plant. Jalapeño, Habanero, Serrano, Fresno, and Anaheim are all fun to grow and use in the kitchen. I don't eat these raw off the plant in the garden! These have varying amounts of heat and spiciness and good flavors. I love to take little bits of Jalapeño or Serrano and put them in my eggs in the morning. All these pepper plants produce lots and lots of peppers, and I always end up with extras. Probably because I don't eat as many of the sweet peppers. For your entire garden, I would recommend three or four varieties of spicy peppers with just one plant each.

PLUMS

The plum has a special place in my heart. My family had a plum tree in the backyard. I grew up in a home with a modest-sized yard with turf, magnolia trees, and juniper (yes, lots of it, but it was eventually taken out). When we moved into the house, there was a walnut tree, and I remember getting that black stuff all over my hands from shelling walnuts. But it was the plum tree right outside the back door that introduced me to wonderful fruit. Every year, we would be blessed with buckets of plums. My mom would make jam, dried fruit rolls, and anything else she could think of with it. It was an annual gift. I have fond memories of peeling plum fruit off of a sheet of wax paper and eating it on the way to swim meets! Sometime after my sister and I left for college, the plums were not eaten enough, and my parents discovered they had a rat affectionately known as the killer rat that would dine on the plums. The tree was taken out, and I think the killer rat went somewhere else!

There are three basic types of plums: European, Japanese, and American. The European plum is most common and used for dried fruit purposes, but it is also eaten fresh. These types of plums grow best in cold climates, as they tend to need chilling hours on the high side—800 to 1,000 hours. If you have any plum trees in your backyard, it is likely a Japanese variety. These plums are more disease resistant and vigorous than a European plant. These trees only require 250–700 chill hours and produce fabulous fruit for fresh eating, juicing, or jam. American plums are commonly crosses of native plums with European or Japanese varieties. These trees do well in cold climates and undesirable soil situations with their American plum rootstocks.

Beautiful plums. Photo by Alina Matveycheva.

Plums have a wide range of ripening possibilities, ranging from early June to mid-October. That is a four-month range; however, the majority of varieties ripen from mid-July to mid-August. Popular varieties for the backyard include Japanese plum cultivars such as Satsuma, Elephant Heart, and Santa Rosa.

***

POMEGRANATES

The pomegranate is a truly ancient fruit hailing from Persia, the Mediterranean, Arabia, Afghanistan, India, and China. As a Bible student, I have come across references to pomegranates many times in the Old Testament, where they represent abundance, faithfulness, and holiness. In the backyard, the pomegranate tree provides tremendous beauty during the fall. Its leaves often turn bright yellow during the fall and the small, oval shapes provide great variety to the structure of your garden. Then, when you see red pomegranates hanging from these trees, they really are spectacular. You almost don't want to pick pomegranates because they look so pretty. But you should pick them when they are that pretty, shiny red. Pomegranates are easy to grow and care for, and they make great landscape screens as they are bushy plants reaching upwards of 15 feet (4.6 m) in height and possibly 10 feet (ca. 3 m) to 12 feet (3.7 m) wide. The tasty part of the pomegranate is the seeds inside the fruit. These are called arils. It is rather challenging to get the little buggers out of the pomegranates to eat, but once you get the hang of it, it is worth the effort. You're actually eating the seeds, which is somewhat unusual. For most fruits, you discard the seed and eat the flesh. But not in pomegranates; you must dig and remove them from all the other stuff.

A harvest of Wonderful variety pomegranates.

Pomegranates are considered one of the healthiest fruits. One cup of those arils supplies you with a healthy dose of fiber, protein, folate, potassium, and vitamins C, E, and K. These little power nuggets are also thought to improve numerous ailments, such as high blood pressure, inflammation, and even bacterial infections.

Pomegranates require low chill hours and do well in hot regions. Not picky about soil and drought tolerant, they will thrive in deep loamy soil. They will need some regular irrigation to get started and to produce fully; however, they can do adequately with low irrigation once established. Make sure to guarantee soil drainage, as these plants won't do well in saturated soil. It is possible to prune pomegranates to a single-trunk tree look, and they naturally seem to grow as a multi trunk bush-type plant. It is advisable to prune them each year during the winter, removing suckers and unnecessary growth. I will be honest; I don't prune my pomegranates much. Maybe a trim here and there.

I have a Dave Wilson Nursery, Wonderful pomegranate that produces large, tasty fruit. This plant is self fruitful, and I harvest it in September and October. I also have two other types of unknown variety!

POTATOES

The potato is high on the list of significant vegetables across the world and is used differently by many cultures. For example, Italy makes gnocchi, Ireland and Great Britain make shepherd's pie, North America uses potatoes in various hot dishes, and many make French fries. Potatoes are a versatile vegetable and can be included in soups, salads, main dishes, side dishes, etc. Potatoes are fat and cholesterol-free vegetables that are also low in sodium and have a high amount of fiber. They are the most common vegetable consumed in the United States.

The Irish Potato Famine just serves to show you how critical potatoes are for some countries. In 1845 in Ireland, potatoes began to grow mold on them. The mold caused a significant number of potatoes to be inedible. The mold problem was fed by the moist conditions, and if you've been to Ireland, you know how wet Ireland is. The issue continued to spread for seven years. Nearly one million people died before the end of the famine in 1852, and many people also fled the country. When the famine subsided, the population of Ireland was significantly reduced, and things with the potato supply eventually got better. Imagine if North America had a potato crop failure. Imagine the impact on the supply of French fries and potato chips. That would be pretty disastrous. Not to make light of the Irish Potato Famine. That was a horrible point in history.

Potatoes are really easy to grow. The potatoes themselves form underground and grow around the roots of the plant, protected from the elements. They are also very productive and can help supply your family with food. For example, one seed potato, which is essentially a small piece of potato, will produce up to ten potatoes. Potatoes need well-drained soil to avoid rotting. Make sure to add organic matter such as compost or leaves before planting, particularly if you have a high amount of clay in your soil. They are also not very frost tolerant and will not deal well with hot weather, so plan accordingly.

The process of planting potatoes is different from most plants, which makes it fun. Potatoes start with a seed. Despite what you may think, it isn't the way it seems. It is a piece of potato. It can be an entire potato if you are planting small fingerling potatoes, or it can be a piece of a potato. Before you put your potato seeds in the ground, they need to produce at least two eyes. The eyes are young sprouts on the potatoes. Or you can wait for them to grow actual shoots. I usually don't have the patience to grow shoots and plant once the eyes develop. I get my seed potatoes for planting either at a supply store, or I use organic potatoes. I cut them into one- or two-inch pieces and let them sit out on a cookie sheet for several days to start to sprout or chit. While those pieces are chitting, the skin of the fresh-cut potato hardens up. This hardening will help protect them when planted.

Harvesting potatoes.

To plant them, you create a ditch about four or five inches (ca. 10 to 13 cm) deep. The ditches should be a few feet apart between rows. Place a potato seed with the eye up in the ditch, approximately 12 inches (ca. 30 cm) apart. Then cover the potato seed with a substantial amount of soil—at least several inches. You will notice sprouts coming up from the ground after several weeks. As the plants grow, rake the soil towards them, mounding the dirt against the plant. This will prevent the sun from hitting your potatoes, which is not ideal. Developing potatoes should not be exposed to sunlight, as they will green up, causing a toxic condition to develop. Keep your soil moist, especially in warm weather.

How do you know when they are ready? The easiest way to tell when your potatoes are ready for harvest is when they blossom. Once your blossoms start to drop and get past due, it is time. To harvest them, I use a garden fork. I make sure to drive the fork a long distance away from the plants and below them to avoid damaging them. I drive up the soil and then pull out the plants. Potatoes should be stored in a cool, dry place away from sunlight. They need airflow and should not be stored in a closed container. The fridge is not ideal for potatoes. That leaves the counter for most of us!

Potatoes are broken into early season, midseason, and late-season types. Early season potatoes can be planted about four weeks prior to the last frost date in the spring. The midseason type can be planted later in July. The late-season type can be planted in August or even as late as the fall. I enjoy growing different colors for variety. I have had significant success with the Yellow Finns, Reds, and Purple Majesties. Yellow Finns are a midseason variety that has yellowish or white flesh. They grow medium-sized potatoes. Red potatoes are also midseason types, and they have thin red skin. There is no need to peel these potatoes and they are delicious in potato salad, egg dishes, etc. Purple Majesties are purple on the outside and the inside. They are very nutritious (most purple vegetables are loaded with antioxidants) and versatile in the kitchen. Plus, they are fun looking!

***

PUMPKINS

Pumpkins are technically squash, but they are worthy of their own category. By now, you have probably figured out that the author is a giant pumpkin-growing fanatic. I wrote a book called *Backyard Big: Growing Atlantic Giant Pumpkins in Your Backyard*. I will do my best to reduce the information, making the pumpkin chapter in this book consistent with the rest of the book. But just saying pumpkins are my favorite...

Everyone is familiar with the pumpkin. A pumpkin says fall and brings the arrival of Halloween. It reminds us of pumpkin-spiced lattes and leaves falling from trees. It provides entertainment as we carve pumpkins for Halloween, and it provides food for our festive feasts. Scientists believe that pumpkins originated in North America about 9,000 years ago. The oldest pumpkin seeds have been found in Mexico and date back to somewhere between 7,000 and 5,550 BC. Pumpkins (along with other forms of squash) were historically important foods among Native Americans.

The story of how pumpkins became symbolic of Halloween in the U.S. is an interesting one. The Irish had a tradition of carving vegetables to scare away evil spirits, and when they migrated to the U.S., they discovered the pumpkin. Thus, the pumpkin became the official fruit celebrating Halloween, and so a tradition was born.

Pumpkins come in all shapes, sizes, and colors. There are miniatures, giants, orange ones, red ones, bumpy ones, and smooth ones. Nevertheless, they are all grown on a vine-like pumpkin plant. Low to the ground, fast growing, bright green, and sort of prickly are pumpkin plants. The pumpkin plant will climb if you let it; however, the height, when grown flat, is between one and two feet (ca. 0.3 to 0.6 m). These plants will grow quickly and will fill a garden patch quickly, making them just plain fun.

Once, I gave some pumpkin seeds from one of my giant pumpkins to someone in town who seemed interested in giving a giant pumpkin a try. I forgot I gave this person seeds and was reminded when he contacted me the following summer in a panic. He needed immediate assistance, as the pumpkin plant was taking over his entire backyard. I paid the gentleman a visit one afternoon, and sure enough, the plant was started in the vegetable patch, growing outside the fenced patch, up the fence, over the fence, and onto the lawn! It was like a true Jack and the Beanstalk story. Fortunately, pumpkins take to pruning well, and we reduced the size of the giant that day.

Pumpkins require a good amount of space to spread out. I recommend planting several plants pointing outward on hills at least three feet (ca. 0.9 m) apart. Pumpkin plants like the heat of summer and should be directly seeded anytime between May and July for an October harvest. For us giant pumpkin growers, we start our seeds indoors in early April. The plants are carefully planted in peat pots in the garden in mid-April. Pumpkins are generally easy to start from seed, and the beginning gardener should fear not. Plant the seeds approximately one inch deep (ca. 2.5 cm) and keep the soil moist. Germination should occur within 10 days.

Soil amended with large amounts of manure is loved by pumpkin plants. These plants are hungry for nutrients, particularly the top three macronutrients (nitrogen, potassium, and phosphorus). Pumpkin plants need lots of water. Roots develop at each node, creating more capacity for growth and energy for your pumpkins.

Several months in, you will notice these pretty yellow flowers. First are the male flowers, and days to weeks later, you will notice yellow flowers with a tiny pumpkin under them. The bees will do their thing and fertilize your pumpkins for you. Or you can hand pollinate them. Atlantic Giant Pumpkin growers often perform specific crosses by hand pollination. Your pumpkins will be ready when they are fully colored and hardened.

The author with a giant pumpkin grown in his backyard in 2023.

For a fun Halloween, I would recommend growing standard field pumpkins. Three or four plants should provide plenty of pumpkins for carving and eating. The Big Mac pumpkin is also a joy to grow. These can get over 100 pounds (ca. 45 kg) and are a fun, manageable pumpkin to grow. Of course, my top recommendation to grow is the true Atlantic Giant Pumpkin. The Atlantic Giant Pumpkin was a selectively bred type of pumpkin started by the father of giant pumpkins, Howard Dill. Before Mr. Dill's specific breeding methods, the largest pumpkin was only several hundred pounds. Mr. Dill's selective breeding opened the door to true giant pumpkins. I am convinced that a complete novice can grow a 500-pound (ca. 227 kg) pumpkin in their first year. They make fantastic conversation pieces and are very fun. The most recent world record for the heaviest pumpkin was set by a man from Minnesota with a weight of 2,749 pounds (ca. 1,247 kg)!

SQUASH

Zucchini is an extremely productive plant. In fact, all squash is equally productive. You put them in the ground thinking they're never going to get started, then the first zucchini comes, you pick it, you eat it, and you enjoy it. Then, soon after, another one comes, and then another and another, all in the same week. You try to keep up, feeding them to your family. Soon, you find newly ripe zucchini nearly every day. You start harvesting the zucchinis that are getting too large before they're too big and get dry and seedy. Then your family gets zucchini fatigue, and you are forced to find another victim. Perhaps a neighbor, friend, or church! Squash, including zucchini, is so productive, and it adds so much to the gardener's confidence because of it.

Even though there are summer and winter squash categories, they're both grown during the summer. The summer squash includes varieties such as zucchini, patty pans, and crookneck. Winter squash can be stored over the winter and includes varieties such as butternut, acorn, and spaghetti squash. Summer squash grows more upright like bushes, and winter squash grows closer to the ground like vines.

Yellow squash. Photo byJulia VeXmedld.

Squash do well in fertile, well-drained soil in hot, sunny locations and are heat loving and sensitive to frost, so they should be planted after the danger of frost has passed. This is between March and June, similar to pumpkins, tomatoes, and other vegetables. As I have indicated previously, I often shy away from March as there are still cold spells that frequently occur, and I would recommend planting these in late April, May, or June. You can start your own plants from seed indoors, sow them directly from seed in your garden, or purchase transplants. Squash is very easy to start from seed. For those sowing the seeds, you can get specific planting depths and particulars on the seed packaging. Squash plants get very large and need lots of space. Perhaps not as much space as melons, but they are close. I like to put these at least three feet (ca. 0.9 m) apart from each other to allow them plenty of space. A family of four only requires two or three squash plants.

Compost and mulch are always helpful, as is fertilizing with an organic fertilizer occasionally. Fertilizer is helpful but not required, especially if you have rich soil. Your plants will need consistent water, preferably in the mornings. Squash plants are susceptible to various pests and diseases, and morning watering and consistently moist soil help prevent disease problems. Powdery mildew seems to be a common issue for me. I have also never had a season without aphids on my squash plants. Insecticidal soap can be very helpful. In addition, slugs and snails seem to like squash plants and can do a lot of damage, especially when the plant is small.

Harvest frequently when the fruit is not too large. This can mean picking zucchini when it is only eight inches (ca. 20 cm) long or patty pans only four inches (ca. 10 cm) to six inches (ca. 15 cm) in diameter. Some summer squash can get thick, hardened skin if you leave it on the plant too long (patty pan, for example). Pick them early! Zucchini grow super fast. Pick them small before they get too big and chewy. My favorite is the Eight-ball. These are round, get the size of a softball, and have good flavor and productivity. Winter squash can stay on the plant longer, and some of them get very hard skin. That is okay; you won't eat the skin anyway.

***

SUNFLOWERS

Sunflowers are easy-growing flowers with edible seeds and are a great annual addition to the backyard. Vincent van Gogh had it right. Sunflowers are beautiful, and they are worthy of a painting. Interestingly, they are native to North America, yet van Gogh painted them in Paris in the late-1800s. There are some 70 types of sunflowers of different sizes and colors. My favorites are the giants, of course. They can reach more than 20 feet tall (ca. 6 m). Another fascinating thing about sunflowers is how they orient toward the sun, tracking it throughout the day. When the sun goes down, the sunflower will even reorient to the east in preparation for sunrise. How do they know?

Sunflower seeds are a healthy food with good fats, vitamins, and minerals and are thought to help prevent heart disease and type II diabetes. One cup of sunflower seeds has 29 grams of protein. That is a lot of protein. You can start planting sunflowers outdoors after the danger of frost has passed. I would suggest April or May. If you have the seed supply, plant a row of sunflower seeds about six inches (ca. 15 cm) apart. They will come up in about a week in good conditions and can be thinned to 18 inches to 24 inches (ca. 0.5 to 0.6 m) apart. Once they grow, sunflowers are fairly drought tolerant, only needing water if it is hot. Depending on the size of your sunflower plants, you may need to offer support.

Giant sunflower, reaching 14 feet, in author's backyard.

Of course, I am most interested in really tall sunflowers. The current world record is more than 30 feet (ca. 9 m) tall! Common types of giant or tall sunflowers include Mammoth, Mongolian Giant, the Skyscraper, and the American Giant Sunflower. The most popular types for planting are Mammoth, Lemon Queen, and Black Oil.

TOMATOES

The tomato is the ultimate vegetable garden crop. Even though the tomato is officially a fruit, it is considered a vegetable by most. How lucky we are! Many put the tomato in the vegetable category, and it raises the reputation of vegetables. Virtually everyone I know plants tomatoes, and many will design their entire summer garden around the tomato. You can find tomatoes in containers on apartment balconies, in significant vegetable gardens, or even in the back forty on bare ground. The tomato is also a great gateway vegetable. It is easy to find success, leading the aspiring gardener to try new vegetables. Tomatoes aren't just red baseball-sized orbs. They come in many shapes, colors, and sizes, from the Mortgage Lifter reaching more than a pound each to the small cherry tomato. There are red tomatoes, yellow tomatoes, black tomatoes, and even striped ones. They all have a unique tomato flavor. Another reason tomatoes are so popular is that they are very useful. You can eat them raw with a little salt and pepper; you can make a tomato salad with balsamic and other vegetables; you can make your own salsa; and, of course, you can make pasta sauce.

Tomatoes. Photo by Bonnie Kittle.

Tomatoes work great in raised-bed vegetable gardens with conditioned soil. They will grow rapidly and not need a lot of care. The plants are so tough that you can even plant them on bare ground in the backyard with unconditioned soil, and they will grow. However, I find that they take well to lots of compost and well-conditioned soil. It is possible to grow them in containers as long as consistent watering is offered. If you are a plant it and leave it gardener, tomatoes in containers may not be the thing for you. They do require consistent watering.

There are two types of tomato plants based on their growth patterns: determinate and indeterminate. Determinate tomatoes have finite growth and ripen in a single batch around the same time. This batch of ripening tomatoes can be spread over weeks or more. Don't let a single ripening deter you. They will provide tomatoes for several weeks or more in most cases, and you can fit a few determinate plants in the space of one indeterminate plant. Indeterminate tomatoes continue to grow and will get very large by season's end. It is not unusual for an indeterminate to get over eight feet (2.4 m) tall if it has adequate support. Yes, indeterminate types will technically produce fruit longer than determinate types. If you're into planting tomatoes that get spectacularly large and creating structures for them, this can be done with indeterminate types. However, I feel that all that vegetation does not necessarily bring more tomatoes. I get much higher yields from determinate types of tomato plants.

Tomatoes can be started from seed fairly easily. They can be sown several months before the season begins. For example, you can start your seeds indoors in February, letting them grow into little tomato plants by April. It is pretty fun to order your seeds online and get them started yourself. It is probably easiest to use grow lights to get them started, depending on your access to the sun in your house. You just can't put these little guys outside when there's frost. Probably the most common way people start tomatoes is with transplants purchased at a nursery and planted directly in the ground in approximately April or May. You can get a pack of seeds for less than five dollars and grow dozens of plants from them, or you can purchase transplants, costing anywhere from $1 each to more than $10 for a large transplant.

To plant your tomatoes, put them deeply in your soil. Pull off the first row or two of leaves and plant deeply up to the remaining leaves. Roots will develop from the stem and from the area on the stem where the leaves were removed. Water them very well after planting, and be sure to keep the soil moist by watering consistently. I make sure to give them a good soak at least once a week and sprinkle several times a week in addition. One word of caution: it is easy to plant them too close together and not realize how big they will get. This is a mistake I often make. If they are too close together, they will grow into each other, making it difficult to find and pick your tomatoes. Your tomato plants will grow very fast. It may take a bit of time to get going if it's cold. Thus, I really recommend you wait until it's plenty warm before you plant them. My best time is sometime in April. Once, I put them in the ground in March and used row covers to keep them warm, and that was successful. If it is too chilly, the plants will just sit in the ground, and you'll wonder: What the heck is this plant doing? Is it resting? Dead?

Eventually, the plants start growing, and they grow quickly. The plants will grow upright, with a primary stem in the center. Secondary branches will grow laterally from the primary stem, and tertiary branches will grow at the junction between the primary and secondary branches. Tertiaries typically won't bear fruit, and some people cut them out. But you will find this task to be very time consuming as your plants grow rapidly. I just let them be! Most tomatoes need cages or some sort of structure to support them. Note that there are commercial tomato plants that grow close to the ground and don't need structure. If you are growing determinate plants, a standard tomato cage works well. The plant will grow inside the cage and then over the top. As the plant gets ripe tomatoes, it will need the cage to support the extra weight. If you are growing indeterminate types, you can build a structure out of various materials. I have used wire, PVC pipe, cattle paneling, etc.

Tomatoes grow vigorously and can withstand most pests well. Watch for the tomato hornworm that begins to appear when your plants are mature. This is a very common pest. It's disgusting and shocking when you see it. You will notice little black dots on the leaves, which are the tomato hornworm poop. You'll see little bits of tomatoes and leaves eaten. In some cases, you can see all of the leaves on branches eaten back to the stem. These can get out of control if you don't stay on top of them. They're actually very difficult to see, as they are the same color as the plant. You have to sit there and watch, and you will notice at one point that there is a large worm-like thing that is green to match the tomato plant, with little teeth on one end and a pooper on the other end. They get several inches long, and they're just gross. Some people will actually grab them by hand and throw them out. I don't even like to touch them. I just cut the branch off with the hornworm on it and throw it in the chicken coop, compost bin, or trash. You'll want to check for hornworms in the morning or evening. They don't come out during the sunny parts of the day. You can even hear them if it's quiet enough, crunching away on your hard-earned tomato plants. Other pests include gophers, which occur occasionally; birds, which will pick at your tomato plants; or even ground squirrels, which will steal your tomatoes. The hornworm is the worst. All other pests occur occasionally, and I am always willing to give a little to those pests. But the hornworm is a different case.

Your tomatoes will typically begin to ripen three to four months after planting. In my area, this is typically in June or July, depending on the weather and how your season has been going. It is said that a watched kettle never boils. This is true for tomatoes. I try not to spend too much time looking. Green tomatoes actually show relatively early, and it is hard to see them as they are the same color as the plant. Once you get your first few red tomatoes, you're off to the races. The greatest thing is when you have so many tomatoes on your plants that you end up having to give them away. Homegrown tomato gifts are the best! Depending on your pest situation (birds, squirrels, raccoons, etc.), you may want to remove the tomatoes as soon as they turn red and let them fully ripen on the counter before a pest gets to them. Make sure to check your plant frequently for ripe tomatoes and pick all the fruit before you get an overripe mess. Rotten tomatoes can bring unsavory pests to your garden, including bugs and rats. As the season slows to an end and you get frost, your plants will naturally slow down. I usually harvest until November. Don't forget if you pick them up as soon as they have a little color, they will ripen on the counter. They must have started to ripen, however. If you still have lots of green tomatoes, you can use them—you can pickle them or fry them!

I typically plant between eight and 12 determinate types of tomato plants. I really like the Ace variety and the Celebrity. These two tomato types will handle most of my needs and will provide more than enough tomatoes for my family of four, as well as giveaways. It provides enough tomatoes for me to actually make salsa several times during the summer and to make spaghetti sauce. It's also fun to plant a few varieties that I've never planted before just to see how they do—different colors, different shapes, different flavors, etc. One year, I planted a yellow tomato that got humongous and had many tomatoes on the plant all summer. I didn't know what to do with all of them. I ended up having to throw many away just because I had so many. I could not believe the productivity of that one tomato plant. Sometimes that just happens.

Chapter Seven

Growing Food Month-by-Month

Pick a month! Whatever month you're in, go to the section below and get started! I have set up a month-by-month schedule on the following pages. There is something to do every month in your garden, whether it's cleaning up from prior months or getting ready for future months. Of course, there is a general cycle of things. You will spend the winter and fall months doing lots of preparation, and the summer months harvesting and caring for your fruits and vegetables. Notice the pronounced changes from month to month and patterns over the year. They tend to be the same every year, with slight adjustments due to the weather. I include average temperatures in the warm Mediterranean Central Valley area of California. It may be necessary to adjust for your local conditions. All weather is local!

Each month has three categories for your consideration. First, you'll find a listing of key gardening and planting tasks. It is essential to plan your garden and plant at the correct time. Second, is a list of fruits and vegetables that are likely to ripen in your garden. The third and final category, is a list of things to do in your fruit and vegetable garden.

JANUARY

January in the Central Valley, California, is marked by cool days and cold evenings. The average high is approximately 52 degrees Fahrenheit (ca. 11 °C), and the average low is 37 degrees Fahrenheit (ca. 3 °C). It is one of the coolest and wettest months of the year. Fruit trees get their needed winter chill, and deciduous trees drop their leaves. It is bare root fruit tree planting time. Check your local nursery for fruit tree supplies, or search the web for bare root jewels and get them ordered. January is also planting season for many vegetables. You can plant asparagus, and beets. You can also plant broccoli and cabbage in most areas. Citrus trees are showing their fruit in January. Oranges, tangerines, limes, lemons, and all types of citrus can be harvested. If you planted broccoli and/or cabbage in the fall, it is possible these could be ready for harvesting. This depends on the weather and your success with the fall garden.

To Do

- Load up the compost bins with leaves.

- Check the garden for standing water and drainage issues.

- Plant bare root fruit trees.

- Plant asparagus, beets, broccoli, and cabbage.

- The soil is likely wet. Avoid digging unless absolutely necessary.

- This month is a good one for dormant fruit tree spraying.

- Onions have been in the ground for several months and could use a shot of fertilizer.

- Harvest citrus.

FEBRUARY

February in California's Central Valley begins to warm up a bit, but it is barely noticeable compared to January in most years. The average high is approximately 55 degrees Fahrenheit (ca. 13 °C), and the average low is 37 degrees Fahrenheit (ca. 3 °C). It is still a good time to plant bare root fruit trees, and fruit trees in the ground are typically dormant. As with January, you can plant asparagus, beets, broccoli, and cabbage. Leaf lettuce can be sown in February. As far as harvesting goes, pick the fruit on your citrus trees, including oranges, tangerines, limes, and lemons. If you planted broccoli and/or cabbage in the fall, and haven't harvested them yet, check to see if they are still edible and then harvest away! If they aren't edible, chop them up with the shovel and toss them in the compost! Depending on your weather, it is possible to use row covers to keep your vegetables a little warmer.

To Do

- Keep gathering leaves and yard debris and adding them to the compost pile.

- The soil is likely wet. Avoid digging unless absolutely necessary.

- Plant asparagus, beets, broccoli, cabbage, and leaf lettuce.

- Start your spring vegetables by seed indoors.

- Some pests get going in February—snails may need to be controlled.

- February's frost is likely. Be prepared to cover sensitive plants.

- Commence fruit tree pruning if the weather permits.

- If you are treating your fruit trees with dormant spray, this month may be a crucial time.

MARCH

Things begin to warm slightly in March, as the average high temperatures in the Central Valley are 57 degrees Fahrenheit (ca. 14 °C) and the average lows are 40 degrees Fahrenheit (4 °C). The weather this time of year can be highly variable, with unannounced frost and relatively warm days. If you are willing to risk it, you can start planting your spring vegetables outdoors. Bare root fruit trees can still be planted during March; however, supply is not ideal at nurseries, and some may be showing signs of waking up from dormancy. If you are not worried about frost and it appears to be a warm March, you can start a variety of spring vegetables and plants, such as lettuce, melons, and even tomatoes. Broccoli, and cabbage, can still be planted at this time if you haven't planted them yet. Depending on when you planted garlic, onions, potatoes, and strawberries, you might have a harvest this month.

To Do

- Finalize your vegetable garden plan.

- This is a good time to amend your garden beds with compost.

- Vegetables started indoors can go outside for acclimation on warm days.

- Plant beets, broccoli, cabbage, and leaf lettuce, and, if you dare, melons and tomatoes.

- Keep an eye on weeds in vegetable beds and pull as needed.

- Consider mulching around fruit trees.

- Check irrigation lines and emitters.

- Finish fruit tree pruning.

- Harvest garlic, onions, potatoes, and strawberries if ready.

APRIL

By April, the chill of winter is disappearing, as average high temperatures in the Central Valley are 65 degrees Fahrenheit (ca. 18 °C) and average lows are 45 degrees Fahrenheit (ca. 7 °C). The soil is warming up, and April is a busy month for gardeners. Citrus should be in the ground at this time, following frost and prior to the heat of summer. You can also plant leaf lettuce, herbs, melons, potatoes and tomatoes. In my opinion, peppers should wait until May; however, many gardeners plant in April. Serious pumpkin growers typically start seeds indoors in early April and plant outdoors in late April. Asparagus is typically harvested in April, as are beets, broccoli, cabbage, garlic, leaf lettuce, potatoes, and ever-bearing strawberries. Both the leaves and bulbs of fast-growing onions can be harvested and eaten immediately.

To Do

- Turn the compost, adding moisture and air to your creation.

- Plant citrus, herbs, leaf lettuce, melons, potatoes, and tomatoes.

- Continue to harden off indoor sown vegetables by putting them outside during warm days.

- Cover vegetable beds with mulch as needed.

- Time to harvest asparagus, beets, broccoli, cabbage, garlic, leaf lettuce, potatoes, and ever-bearing strawberries.

MAY

The sunshine officially arrives full time in May in the Central Valley, with average highs at 74 degrees Fahrenheit (ca. 23 °C) and average lows at 52 degrees Fahrenheit (ca. 11 °C). May typically has more stable weather than March and April, and the soil is usually considerably warmer. You can still plant citrus in May, as well as leaf lettuce, herbs, melons, peppers, potatoes, and tomatoes. Nearly all types of cucurbits (pumpkins, squash) can be planted outdoors in May. May is exciting for fruit growers, as several varieties are typically ripe for harvest. The first to ripen in my backyard are typically cherries, followed closely by apricots and peaches. Blueberries will begin ripening in May as well. Vegetables ready for harvest include garlic, onions, broccoli, cabbage, potatoes, and ever-bearing strawberries.

To Do

- Vegetable beds should be weed free and ready for planting.

- Plant herbs, leaf lettuce, melons, peppers, potatoes, tomatoes, squash, and pumpkins.

- If potatoes are growing, consider earthing them up during May.

- Keep an eye on fruit trees for pests and treat as necessary.

- Consider covering blueberries and cherries with bird netting if you want to taste this fruit in the future.

- Begin routine fruit tree irrigation.

- Check apricots for ripeness.

- Harvest beets, broccoli, cabbage, onions, and potatoes.

JUNE

With June comes warm weather and a considerable increase in temperatures. Average highs reach 85 degrees Fahrenheit (ca. 29 °C) and lows average 61 degrees Fahrenheit (ca. 16 °C) in the Central Valley of California. It is still possible to plant a number of vegetables and herbs as the heat of summer gets rolling, including cucumbers, potatoes, pumpkins, herbs, leaf lettuce, potatoes, tomatoes, and squash. You can also plant ever bearing and day-neutral strawberries in June. There is a good variety of fruits and vegetables ready for harvest. Some apple varieties ripen as early as June, and apricots and blueberries continue to appear throughout the month. Cucumbers, potatoes, and day-neutral strawberries ripen during June. Depending on the variety, peaches and plums may be available for harvest.

To Do

- Remove the fallen fruit to avoid attracting pests.

- Plant cucumbers, pumpkins, herbs, leaf lettuce, potatoes, tomatoes, and squash.

- Feed vegetables with organic fertilizer.

- Walk the garden frequently in the early morning or evening, searching for pests. Treat accordingly.

- June is a big month for apricot harvesting.

- Harvest, harvest, harvest.

JULY

When July arrives, people (and some plants) are already tired of the heat, as temperatures peak in the Central Valley at a high of 94 degrees Fahrenheit (ca. 34 °C) and the average low of 68 degrees Fahrenheit (ca. 20 °C). It is hot, dry, and not uncommon for daytime temperatures to go over 100 degrees Fahrenheit (ca. 38 °C). Take special care to provide adequate water and shade for some plants. I find my peppers, pumpkins, and tomatoes begin to take off during July. It is possible to plant a July garden of broccoli, cabbage, and cauliflower. In addition, it is still possible to plant cucumbers, pumpkins, potatoes, squash, and day-neutral strawberries for the fall harvest. July is harvesting time for plenty of vegetables and fruit, depending on the variety. For example, early apples might appear, as well as plums and strawberries. Apricots are often still on the trees, and peaches, nectarines, and plums are ripening quickly. Ripe tomatoes, peppers, cucumbers, and squash are typically plentiful during July. Don't forget about herbs, which are typically ready for harvest in July.

To Do

- Keep caring for and adding to the compost pile.

- Plant broccoli, cabbage, cauliflower, cucumbers, pumpkins, potatoes, squash, and straw-berries.

- Thin, heavy crops of fruit, such as apples and plums.

- Special care is needed to ensure plants are hydrated during heat waves.

- Provide plenty of water for your vegetables and fruit trees as they are actively growing.

- Harvest cucumbers, herbs, peppers, potatoes, squash, and tomatoes if ready.

AUGUST

August is marked by a slightly lower average temperature during the day in the Central Valley of 92 degrees Fahrenheit (ca. 33 °C) and an average low at night of 67 degrees Fahrenheit (ca. 19 °C). There are fewer opportunities to plant during August; however, that is okay because there is lots of harvesting and cleanup this month. The broccoli, cabbage, and cauliflower planting can continue, and leaf lettuce can be added to the list. Beets can also be sown during this time. Many fruits are at or close to their peak harvest dates, including apples, pears, peaches, nectarines, plums, and hybrids. Herbs, melons, onions, potatoes, pumpkins, tomatoes, and strawberries are ready for picking.

To Do

- Clean up and dispose of fallen fruit.

- Plant beets, broccoli, cabbage, cauliflower, and leaf lettuce.

- Consider pruning fruit trees in the summer to control their size.

- Harvest fruits and vegetables.

SEPTEMBER

Finally, the intense heat of the summer begins to diminish, and fall officially arrives on September 22. Average highs are 86 degrees Fahrenheit (ca. 30 °C), and average lows are 61 degrees Fahrenheit (ca. 16 °C) during this month. It is possible to get an early planting of garlic in, and this continues to be a good time for leaf lettuce. Broccoli, cabbage, and cauliflower can be planted; however, they are nearing the end of the planting window. Peppers, tomatoes, squash, and melons should still be arriving in high quantities for harvest. Fruit harvest is dominated by apples, grapes, and pears, with new appearances of ripe pomegranates. Wine grape harvest is a popular activity during September in the Central Valley.

To Do

- Get rotten tomatoes off the ground.

- Pick and store fruit before it drops from the trees or attracts pests.

- Plant beets.

- Harvest potatoes and store them for later use.

- Check for tomato hornworms and handpick them.

- Harvest fruit.

OCTOBER

October in the Central Valley is marked by average highs of 72 degrees Fahrenheit (ca. 22 °C) and average lows of 51 degrees Fahrenheit (ca. 11 °C). Leaves begin to change color, and pumpkins turn orange in time for Halloween. This month is also marked by a continued wine grape harvest in the Central Valley. You can plant asparagus, beets, garlic, leaf lettuce, and onions. June-bearing strawberries are also planted in October. The late-summer broccoli, cabbage, and cauliflower are approaching harvest time in October. Ever-bearing strawberries, peppers, pomegranates, grapes, and late apples are also harvested.

To Do

- Begin collecting leaves for the compost pile.

- Get onion beds ready by working in compost.

- Cut down the asparagus fern shoots.

- Plant asparagus, beets, blueberries, garlic, leaf lettuce, and onions.

- Start harvesting pomegranates before they split during wet weather.

NOVEMBER

In most years, November marks the beginning of more frequent rain. High temperatures average 58 degrees Fahrenheit (ca. 14 °C), and lows average 41 degrees Fahrenheit (ca. 5 °C) as the fall chill begins to settle in. Early November is onion transplant time in my garden. November is also a good time to plant asparagus, garlic, leaf lettuce, and June-bearing strawberries This would also be the time to harvest the last of the herbs. Most vegetables are slowing down in November, and there is not much of a harvest, with the exception of beets and leaf lettuce.

To Do

- Collect leaves for compost piles or leave them in beds as mulch.

- Remove vegetables that have finished for the year and put them in the compost pile.

- Plant asparagus, garlic, onions, and leaf lettuce.

- Plant blueberries and strawberries for the summer harvest.

- Harvest beets and leaf lettuce.

DECEMBER

The winter chill sets in during December in the Central Valley. Daytime highs are an average of 50 degrees Fahrenheit (ca. 10 °C), and nighttime lows average 36 degrees Fahrenheit (ca. 2 °C). Fruit trees are entering dormancy at this time of year, and everything is quiet in the garden. Bare root berries will be showing up at nurseries during December and can be planted. Beets, broccoli, and cabbage may still be in the garden for harvest, and some citrus may be ready for an early harvest. Leaf lettuce, the mainstay, is the only other significant plant that can be harvested at this time.

To Do

- Cover compost piles during rain to avoid soggy compost.

- Plant blueberries and strawberries.

- Dormant fruit tree pruning is possible in December if it is dry.

- Start dormant fruit tree spraying.

- Harvest citrus if it is ripe.

- Harvest all the beets, broccoli, cabbage, and leaf lettuce.

Chapter Eight

Sowing, Planting, and Ripening Months

To assist with your gardening planning, I have prepared two charts. The first chart depicts the approximate times of seed sowing and planting of select fruits and vegetables in the Central Valley, California. Reminder, timing differs depending on planting by seed or transplant. Appropriate sowing times are indicated by seeds in the chart. Transplant times are indicated by leaves. The second chart depicts the approximate time of ripening of fruits and vegetables. Dark areas are the main ripening window, and gray areas are less frequent ripening periods.

Sowing and Planting Chart

	Jan	Feb	Mar	Apr	May	Jun	Jul	Aug	Sep	Oct	Nov	Dec
Apple	🍃	🍃	🍃	🍃							🍃	🍃
Apricot	🍃	🍃	🍃	🍃							🍃	🍃
Asparagus	🍃	🍃	🍃	🍃	🍃				🍃	🍃	🍃	
Beets			•	•				•	•	•	•	
Blueberry	🍃	🍃	🍃	🍃							🍃	🍃
Broccoli	🍃	🍃	🍃	🍃	🍃	🍃	•	🍃	🍃	🍃	🍃	
Cabbage	🍃	🍃	🍃	🍃	🍃	🍃	•	🍃	🍃	🍃	🍃	
Cauliflower							•	🍃	🍃	🍃	🍃	
Cherry	🍃	🍃	🍃								🍃	🍃
Citrus				🍃	🍃	🍃	🍃					
Cucumber			•	🍃	🍃	🍃	🍃	🍃	🍃	🍃		
Garlic								🍃	🍃	🍃	🍃	🍃
Grape		🍃	🍃	🍃								
Herbs			•	🍃	🍃	🍃	🍃	🍃	🍃			
Lettuce (leaf)		•	•	🍃	🍃			•	•	🍃	🍃	
Melon			•	🍃	🍃	🍃	🍃	🍃				
Onion									🍃	🍃	🍃	🍃
Peach/Nect.	🍃	🍃	🍃	🍃							🍃	🍃
Pear	🍃	🍃	🍃	🍃							🍃	🍃
Pepper			•	🍃	🍃	🍃	🍃	🍃	🍃	🍃		
Plum	🍃	🍃	🍃	🍃							🍃	🍃
Pomegranate	🍃	🍃	🍃	🍃							🍃	🍃
Potato				🍃	🍃	🍃	🍃	🍃	🍃	🍃	🍃	
Pumpkin					•	🍃	🍃	🍃	🍃			
Squash					•	🍃	🍃	🍃	🍃			
Tomato			•	🍃	🍃	🍃	🍃	🍃				

Ripening Chart

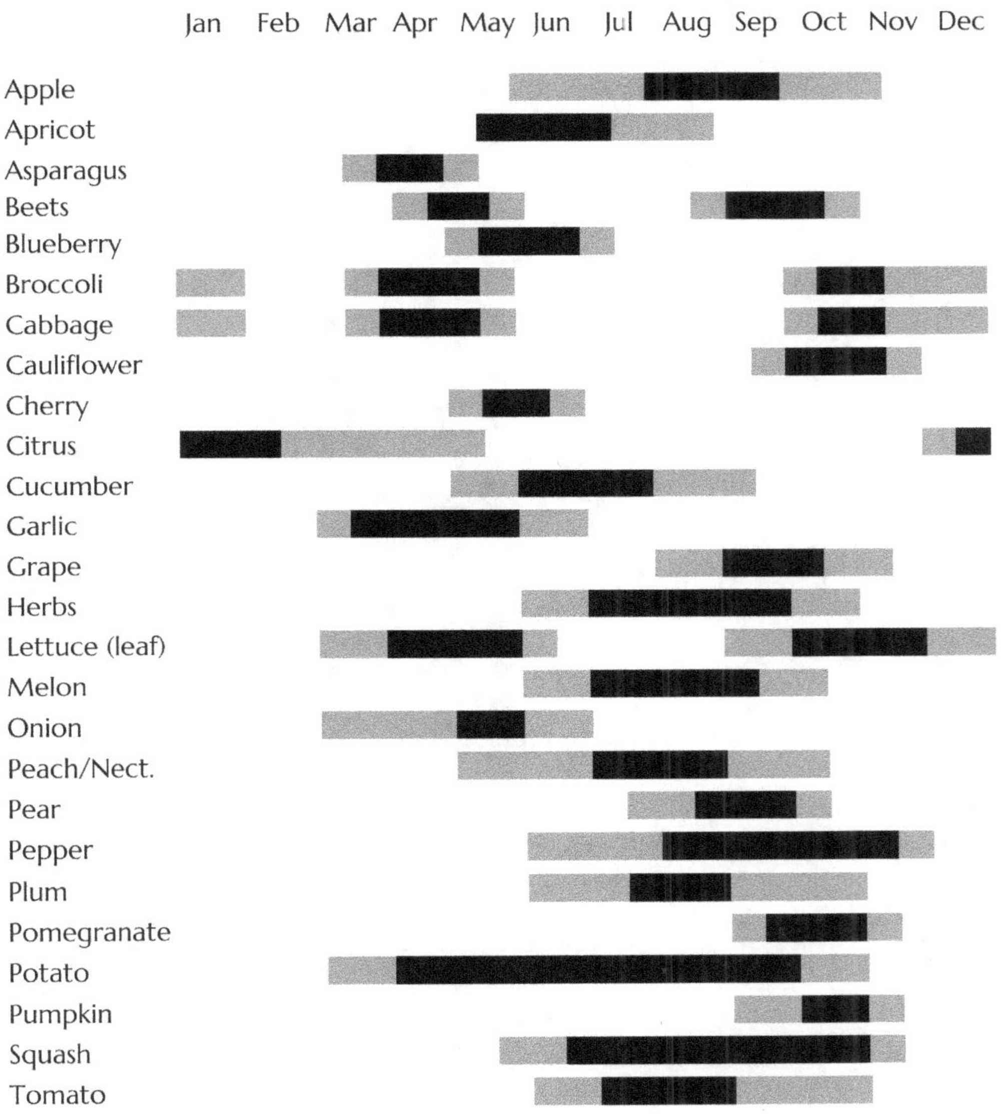